DON'T BE

S.A.D.

A TEENAGE GUIDE TO HANDLING
STRESS, ANXIETY & DEPRESSION

SUSAN NEWMAN

Julian Ⓜ Messner

© 1991 by Susan Newman

Photographs © 1991 by George Tiboni

Cover photograph: © Comstock Inc./Peter D'Angelo

Published by Julian Messner, a division of Silver Burdett Press, Inc., Simon & Schuster, Inc., Prentice Hall Building, Englewood Cliffs, NJ 07632.

JULIAN MESSNER and colophon are trademarks of Simon & Schuster, Inc.
Design by Michael J. Freeland
Manufactured in the United States of America

Lib. ed. 10 9 8 7 6 5 4 3 2 1

Pbk. ed. 10 9 8 7 6 5 4 3 2 1

Library of Congress Cataloging-in-Publication Data

Newman, Susan.
    Don't be S.A.D. : a teenage guide to handling stress, anxiety & depression / Susan Newman : photographs by George Tiboni.
        p. cm.
    Includes bibliographical references and index.
    Summary: Presents case histories of teenagers who have problems with stress, anxiety, or depression. Discusses techniques for dealing with these emotions.
    1. Adjustment (Psychology) in adolescence—Juvenile literature. 2. Stress in adolescence—Juvenile literature. 3. Anxiety in adolescence—Juvenile literature. 4. Anxiety in adolescence—Case studies—Juvenile literature. 5. Depression in adolescence—Juvenile literature. 6. Depression in adolescence—Case studies—Juvenile literature. [1. Stress (Psychology) 2. Anxiety. 3. Depression.] I. Tiboni, George, ill. II. Title. III. Title: Don't be sad.
    BF724.3.A32N48   1991
    158'.1'0835—dc20   91-24471
                                                                                CIP
                                                                                 AC

ISBN 0-671-72610-2 (LSB)
ISBN 0-671-72611-0 (pbk.)

CONTENTS

For every teenager who is faced with the uncertainty of how to deal with problems and emotions . . . and for Lillian Spina-Caza, who created the S.A.D. concept as a source of guidance and support

ACKNOWLEDGMENTS

Stress, anxiety, and depression are complex and closely intertwined issues that were sorted out for this book in part by people who are experts in their fields, and who work with teenagers on a daily basis to help them solve problems. Further clarification of the issues and firsthand insights into the turmoil of the often painful adolescent years were supplied by teenagers themselves.

The case histories presented here are factual; only names, places, and certain identifying characteristics have been changed. I am grateful to the young men and women who, in spite of difficulty in telling their stories, allowed me into their lives and shared the details of their very personal conflicts. The nine stories in this book were chosen from some fifty interviews in order to address as many areas of teen apprehension and emotional difficulty as possible.

The people photographed for these stories are in no way related to the actual subjects or to the circumstances in which those subjects appear. The models were selected rather to portray the real characters on the basis of their ability to convey certain key elements of each subject, primarily that character's personality and feelings. Those pictured in the roles of parents, siblings, officials, and friends are also acting.

To all who agreed to be photographed, who willingly posed as someone they were not, thank you. You have given this book a visual dimension that would not otherwise have been possible.

Several people were vital to the development of this work. Kathy S. Collins, a psychiatric social worker who specializes in adolescent concerns, deserves special thanks. She shared her extensive knowledge with me and read the manuscript with compassion and a keen understanding of teenage life. Sincere thanks are due also to Sue Morrow, the prevention and intervention supervisor of the Hunterdon County [New Jersey] Drug Awareness Program, who offered astute perceptions of teens in distress and repeatedly volunteered her skills and resources. Ellen De Shazo, Coordinator for Maternal Child Health, Adolescent Pregnancy Services, of the Department of Health in Flemington, New Jersey, brought to this book her expertise on teen pregnancy and its long-term ramifications.

Among others who each in his or her own way proved invaluable, either in contributing information essential to the usefulness of the text or in arranging facets of the photography were: Adrienne A. Peck, John Novak, William McDuffie, and Meredith Varga. Nancy Toff expertly edited and guided the manuscript to its final form.

PREFACE

DON'T BE S.A.D.

*M*any adults seem to believe that if a teenager is not moody and miserable he or she is not progressing at the business of growing up. Not true. Being S.A.D.—that is, *s*tressed, *a*nxious, or *d*epressed (any one of which could make a person moody and miserable)—is not a prerequisite for maturity.

It is in fact perfectly possible to have a happy, eventful life from age twelve to twenty while maturing along the way. Nor is it necessary to be in constant conflict with your parents, feel miserable about yourself, or have difficulties with friends. However, because life is pretty complicated these days, it will be harder than it was for your parents to get all the way through these high-risk years without running into some hitches.

One teenager, Sean Weaver, notes that "you're a kid until you're about eleven, then you have to start growing up. Everyone is driven because it is so hard to make it in the world." With the help of the true stories in this book, the problems you face will either be reduced in intensity, fully resolved, or even avoided entirely. In any case, "making it in the world" will be a whole lot easier after you have read them.

As you read, you are going to get a healthy understanding of stress, anxiety, and depression, fancy words that are often tossed around lightly by friends and parents. You may even find yourself using them. But they are, in fact, big words for serious conditions that can make anyone unhappy.

Ever heard the expression "These are the best years of your life"? If you still haven't, you will. When an older person says this to you, it's okay to snicker. Adults often manage to forget what their own growing years were like. They have long memories for the high spots—the first dance they attended, or their first kiss. Their memories are short, though, for the times they thought their worlds were disintegrating—the dance they missed, the club they weren't invited to join, the important track meet they lost.

On top of their faded and selective memories, a lot of parents don't realize that there have been changes that make our society quite different from the one in which they were raised. Now drugs are truly everywhere. More teenagers also try alcohol than ever did before. It is not uncommon to see high-school freshmen passed out drunk at parties weekend after weekend. More teenagers are sexually active, but they do have one advantage over their parents: they can talk openly about sex.

"Everyone has the opportunity to know everything," as fifteen-year-old Kay Brooker from Kansas City says. "There is no reason for anyone to be ignorant about any form of sexual pressure from date rape to venereal diseases or about drugs from alcohol, steroids, and marijuana to heroin addictions. The information is out there.

"There are so many more clinics that aren't ashamed of what they do. There are pamphlets, books, movies, television shows, and documentaries. The yellow pages have listings of people to talk to," adds Brooker. "Unlike our parents' generation, we admit that there are pressures and discuss them."

Today, teenage pregnancy no longer shocks. "I don't even turn around anymore at school when a pregnant student passes me in the hall," says Meredith Owen, a high-school junior. "Last spring a girl left school seven months pregnant. She returned in the fall, the mother of twins."

Early on, the pressure mounts to do well in school. More and more teenagers have come to realize that a college education is very important, a necessity for many jobs. With that realization comes more intense competition to gain a place in the college of your choice. And in addition to school pressures, about one-third of all teenagers have part-time jobs.

Almost everywhere in our country there is a feeling of rushing, of racing to succeed and to have more money. Your parents may be swept up in this competition, pursuing their careers and perhaps muddling through a divorce. Because they may be heavily involved with their own problems, they may often have limited time for you. High-school senior Tim Clark expains what can happen: "My friend's mother was shocked when the teacher called to tell her that her son was doing poorly in his calculus class. His mother said, 'I didn't know he was taking calculus.' "

Fourteen-year-old Elizabeth Minkovitz confirms that "a lot of my friends' parents are out of touch with their children's lives." If you have a parent who doesn't know what you are doing in school or socially, you will need to make a bigger effort to set your own limits.

"I have a curfew and a set amount of time for talking on the phone," adds Elizabeth. "I think it's better to have restrictions to hold me together. Most of the guys don't have curfews. I have the earliest one for my age, but it's not a problem for me."

Whether or not they have specified limits, most teenagers today are less protected and less coddled by their parents and teachers. Yet both expect more of teenagers than ever before. Living up to their expectations and the ones you've created for yourself can be rough, particularly if those expectations are set too high. In so many ways you may be asked to assume more responsibility than you may want or may be ready for. For example, you may have to supervise younger brothers and sisters or do the cooking more often than you would like or think fair. At the very least, most teens today are expected to act grown up, which is a pressure in itself.

Being adult and being a child at the same time can be very confusing and very *un*satisfying. On the one hand, you must fend for yourself and be on your own. On the other hand, many parents have a hard time giving their children over to themselves. They may say they want to trust you, but it often seems as if they trust you only as far as they can see you. It is the rare parent who takes his teenager seriously.

During the teen years you are trying to define who you are. You know you are somewhere between being a kid and an adult. There are many new events to capture your interest. There are boys . . . and girls. Some of the new opportunities and situations you will have to face can be fun, but some will be scary. Your values are changing, too. So if you feel confused, you are more than entitled. Some misery during the teen years is normal. So much is changing in your life, starting with your body and culminating with wanting to be your own person, to run your own life. Even your personality is changing. You probably have stronger views, and stronger likes and dislikes now. Your desires may conflict with what your parents want for you or that they imagine you want for yourself. In their efforts to be good parents, those who have the time may invade your privacy and not understand your needs. Now, when you are fighting to gain control over your life it's infuriating when they act as if you can't dress yourself.

Clashes with parents should happen now and then. Your opinions are bound to be different from those of people around you. The closer you are to a parent, the more likely you are to differ on any number of issues. Arguing with your parents means that they care enough to worry about you. Contrary to what most of us think, these differences of opinion reflect a strong attachment. This tie is not a sign of immaturity or of inability to stand on one's own two feet.

There will probably be times you're in a rage, so angry at your parents that you cannot think straight. At such times they will seem to be telling you what to do without asking what you want to do. Your anger may well be justified. Your parents may not seem to approve of anything you do, and you may feel sure that their actions prove they don't love you. You feel as if you're a failure at everything you try. There will be days when you feel left out or ignored by your friends, overpowered by your parents, and angry at the entire world. Feelings that life has handed you a raw deal, that life is unfair, that you have too many people to please and too much to do, overwhelm everyone occasionally. And there may be days when just the act of thinking is too difficult to undertake.

Feeling glum or as if you're living under the crust of a volcano that's about to erupt should be only an occasional state, not one you experience with annoying regularity. If you're stressed out most of the time or anxious about situations that should be easy to handle, you need to find out why, then do something about whatever is making you unhappy.

In these pages you will discover techniques to help you over rocky roads you may be encountering. You will not see yourself in every one of these case histories, but you will most likely know someone who is—or has been—in a similar predicament. You will learn about your own feelings and be able to take command of your own life. The sections that follow each story, called "Facts to Focus On" and "Moving in the Right Direction," will pinpoint what may be bothering you and suggest ways to correct it.

It can be embarrassing to ask for help from parents or from people trained to help you. This book will get you over the uncomfortable spots without forcing you to advertise your feelings. It will also help you size up a problem and put it in proper perspective.

Ignoring a serious problem will cause or increase stress, anxiety, and depression. There are some things we simply cannot fix by ourselves. And the things we're talking about have a way of growing and getting out of hand. It's not easy to talk about personal problems—but if you let them slide, a chain reaction can occur. Problems that are ignored can pile up as quickly as cars on an icy freeway. You wouldn't attempt to fix your own broken bone, so why try to end a depression by yourself? And you wouldn't take out your own appendix, so why think you can stop your parents from drinking, fighting, or abusing each other or you?

There are in fact problems that you can correct. If you are doing poorly in school, you can improve. If you get caught up in the drug scene, only you can stop using drugs (although you may need help here). If you are pushing yourself too hard, only you can pull back.

No one sails through the growing-up process, but you can reduce much of its "S.A.D.ness" by making life more pleasant for yourself whenever you can. No one feels very good about himself if he is saddled with annoying problems. When you get rid of some of them, you'll feel much better about yourself, and things that once seemed insurmountable will become easy. Be patient. When you think that your world is self-destructing, bear in mind that, given time, most situations change or can be changed. Anything is possible. Believe in yourself. You can be a teenager and get a solid grip on who you are and what you're doing. Don't be S.A.D. You don't have to be.

PART I

DON'T BE STRESSED

*Y*ou know you're under stress; everyone is. Stress is part of life. But how much is too much? This stress test will give you some idea of how stressed out you are. Think before you answer, and be honest with yourself.

1. Do you bit your nails, or pick at your cuticles?
2. Do you have a habit of touching your eyes, nose, or ears? Of twisting a strand of hair?
3. Do you stutter all the time? Or only when you're nervous?
4. Are you tired for no reason (not because you stayed up late doing homework or talking with a friend)?
5. Do you skip meals?
6. Do you have frequent headaches?
7. Do you have stomachaches that can't be linked to eating junk food or overeating?
8. Do you agree to do everything that is asked of you?
9. Do you rarely laugh or have fun?
10. Does your skin break out in rashes or hives for what seems to be no reason—that is, you are not having an allergic reaction?
11. Do you have trouble falling asleep at bedtime? Or do you wake up in the middle of the night? Do you have nightmares?
12. Do you lose your temper quite often?

If you answered yes to any of these questions, you are experiencing some degree of stress that needs attention.

People feel stressed when the pressures and demands on them are too many or too strong. You may be under stress and not realize it, because you never actually knew what stress was. Stress is anything that puts you under so much strain that you react somehow. The reaction may be either physical (your hands sweat, your head feels strange, your stomach is upset) or emotional (you worry or feel nervous). The pressure—whether it comes from parents, teachers, or friends—can put you in conflict or worry you. Maybe you want to meet the demands but maybe you don't . . . or can't because you don't know how.

Very often, isolating the cause of the stress—identifying the stressor—is step one. Once you know what is causing stress, you can change it, get rid of it, begin to approach it in a different way or, at the very least, think about it differently.

Teens who are not "stress savvy" make life more difficult for themselves. By increasing your stress knowledge you will become able to dispose of stressors you don't need. The ones you can't dismiss you can learn to deal with more easily. As you do so, your signs of stress will begin to vanish.

Stress strikes in different forms. One person may find the pressure to get straight A's quite manageable, another might put himself in a state of panic over the same goal. Someone else could thrive under circumstances that make your legs itch and your heart beat so fast that it feels as if it will pop out of your chest.

You may find the mere idea of getting on a Ferris wheel enough to make your legs shake. If the class trip is planned for an amusement park, worrying about the rides can keep you upset—that is, under stress—until that event is finally over. On the other hand, your best friend may think that a roller coaster with anything less than hair-raising dips and rocketing speed is for babies. This close friend is a thrill seeker and more of a risk taker than you are. For him the class trip will be a much-anticipated event. The point is: how you view a situation determines the amount of stress you feel in it and whether or not it is good for you.

STRESS—THE GOOD AND THE BAD

In certain situations and for certain people, stress is good because it can motivate you and help you achieve goals. Take Steve Jensen, for example. Steve plays baseball for his school. Before a game, he gets completely worked up. By the start of the game, he feels as if he can beat the other team all by himself. Steve is a case of stress working for you.

Good stress can also act as a personal alarm. It can tell you when you may be in danger. Stress that alerts you can help you win a race by telling you that a competitor is gaining on you. The stress of a test can spur you to study harder, with the result that you get a better grade.

Stress can work against you, too. Nicole Yee is very smart: she answers questions in class that no one else can. But when it's time for a written test, Nicole falls apart. The night before an exam, she has nightmares about historical battles or complex equations, depending on the upcoming test's topic. The stress she puts on herself to do well is so enormous that on written tests she confuses her answers and gets terrible grades.

RECOGNIZING WHAT STRESSES YOU

Stress is often caused by a change in your life. For instance, your developing—or developed—body may seem awkward to you. You may spend lots of time figuring out how to hide parts you don't like or don't think look good. Just worrying about how you look is stressful. Moving to a new house, having a parent lose his or her job, being overlooked for an honor, or not being given a place on the team are some unanticipated changes that can create stress.

The pressure to pass tests may also cause you stress. So can worrying about whether someone is going to ask you to a dance. A coach who demands that you improve your performance can set your nerves on edge. Here are a few other things that often keep teens stressed, some more than others:

Parents' rules
Parents' expectations
Teachers' and coaches' expectations
A lack of friends, or working at making new ones
Trying to keep too many friends happy
Schoolwork and college-entrance tests
Quitting school
Doing well at a part-time job and having enough time to complete schoolwork
An unacceptable change in personal appearance, such as acne, weight, height, protruding ears, or braces
A desire to be popular
Wanting to get excellent grades

The hope or dream of being the best at something
Wanting a boyfriend/girlfriend; not wanting a boyfriend/girlfriend
Fighting with siblings
Hassling with parents; parents hassling with each other
Being sick

CHANGING A STRESSFUL SITUATION

Much of what upsets you can be altered to make it less stressful. In your house, for example, there may be rules left over from your elementary-school days. Your parents may not have realized that some of them have become outdated. Don't try bending the rules on your own. It's much more effective to ask your folks to rethink a rule or lighten a restriction. Asking is almost guaranteed to result in having the rule changed in your favor. But if you break a rule to have it your way, the price will usually be punishment or stricter enforcement of the rule.

Approach your parents with a specific revision in mind, one that is realistic. If you want a curfew extended, don't begin by asking for two extra hours. The first time you ask, go for an extra half hour. Be sure to explain why you need more time. Provide a sound reason. Maybe it takes more time than parents think to work on a project with a friend or a dance ends later than they thought it would, or you are traveling farther on your next outing, so it will take longer to get back. Bring up the subject at a calm time of day, not when your parents are frantic to get to work or are in the midst of preparing dinner. Try during dinner or after the dinner dishes have been cleaned up.

You can also change a stressful situation by avoiding it completely. Suppose, for example, that you play soccer but you are secretly afraid each time you face the defense. Every time the ball is on your foot and the crowd yells "Take it all the way!" you pass it to a teammate. Then the crowd groans, and you feel awful. Soccer may not be your game. Consider giving it up for a sport in which you do not have to confront other people. Swimming or gymnastics may be for you instead.

You have the option of fighting the stressor. You can stay out on the soccer field, for instance, and force yourself to keep moving toward the goal. Keep meeting your opponents head on, until clashing on the field no longer bothers you. This approach works for some people, but not for everyone.

Another thing that creates stress is pursuing an interest for the wrong reasons: because your parents want you to, because so much money has already been invested in equipment and lessons, or because your friends are involved. If you regularly wake up in the morning feeling as if you don't want to run a meet, throw a basketball, swim a lap, play a musical piece, or participate in some other activity, you may not truly want to be involved in it any more. (But you should also distinguish between a temporary discouragement and a true lack of interest.)

Continuing something that you don't like doing just to save face or keep your parents happy is ignoring what you want. If you continue with something you don't like, you are not taking the best care of yourself. Signs of stress will eventually crop up. Think it through. Talk it out with a friend. Letting yourself down is a far worse problem than letting down your parents or friends. They have their own lives to worry about. This one is yours.

CHANGING YOUR THINKING

Another way to cope with a stressful circumstance is to begin thinking differently about the stressor. Adopt a new attitude. Let's say you are terrified of a particular teacher. Think about why this is so. Recognize that he is only a person who yells loudly. He is probably a father, a family man. He does not beat his students. What is the worst thing he can do to you? Give you a poor grade. The whole class knows he's tough; he gets some kind of thrill out of embarrassing his students. You are worried that you will be the next one he singles out. The thing to do is to make up your mind that you can stand it. Other students have lived through his rages. You will, too. Once you decide that no matter what this teacher does you will come out okay in the end, the threat will seem less significant. The stress of attending his class will slowly disappear.

Let's say your dad is on your back to clean up the garage, which looks as if the school's entire marching band had camped there for a year. You can't stand to listen to him anymore. To avoid your father, you have started eating dinner early and studying in your room with the door closed. But now you're worried as much about his wrath as you are about simply doing the job.

The solution is to think "I can do it" instead of "I can't." Break the project into manageable parts. Attack one corner of the garage at a time. Ask a friend to help, then offer to help him with something he has to do. Pick the worst part of the job, and do it first. If you change your mindset to "I can do it" a little bit each day, you won't feel as pressured.

If you have been home from school ill, whether it's for a few days or a couple of weeks, the assignments can really accumulate. Instead of panicking, ask your teachers when you return to school to set reasonable deadlines to let you make up the work. If you have proven yourself to be a reliable student, teachers are likely to ask you to do less of the required work or to give you more time to do it. Don't try to do it all at once. Instead of feeling stressed, adopt the attitude that if you work steadily you will catch up sooner or later.

Let's look at another common, but stressful, situation that you may want to start thinking about in a new way. Being popular is something that concerns people of any age. At some point—right now, in fact—it's good to realize that not everyone is going to like you, not everyone is going to be your friend. You're older, though, and can afford to be choosy about friends. It's much more fun, and far less taxing, to be with people who have the same interests you do. If you're into art, you're not likely to choose the star of the hockey team as your best friend. In other words, don't pretend to be someone you are not, simply so that people will like you. That creates enormous strain and is not terribly rewarding in terms of friendships.

You may in fact be different from everyone else you know. You may not fit in with any of the crowd at your school. You're just different, maybe because you're brighter than the other kids or more talented in some way. You can certainly opt to be a loner, as sixteen-year-old Kathleen Barker did. "I'd rather go to the library—although I'm not a geek—and get something done than sit around wasting time with the so-called 'in' crowd," she says. "If the other kids don't like it, too bad. I'm never rude, but I'm just not fake."

Kathleen's choice is fine, if you don't feel stress about going it alone until you find the right people to be your friends. The world would be a very boring place if we were all cheerleaders or football stars.

1.

WHEN THE FUN STOPS

"Your tests show nothing. If the pains don't stop

by late afternoon, we will have to perform an

appendectomy. There is something very

wrong," the doctor told Cindy Cornell.

*C*indy, *a high school junior, is always tired from her hectic and strenuous schedule. She speaks rapidly when she fills you in on the details.*

I'm up at 5:30 to get ready for school and study. School starts at 7:20 and is over at 2:15. After school I have band practice first, then ride the bus to swim practice. I get home at about 7:30, eat dinner, and go to choir practice two nights a week. On choir nights I'm back home about 9:30. I do some homework and talk on the telephone. That's why I have to get up so early. I need extra time in the morning to finish my homework. But I couldn't give up talking to my friends at night.

I've been in band and swimming since grade school. It was easier in elementary school, because I didn't have as much homework *[Cindy takes all honors and advanced placement courses for college]*, and friends weren't as important as they are now. Then I could swim, come home, eat dinner, and go to bed. Now I have tons of homework.

The hassle almost takes away the pleasure. If I miss a practice to write a paper, I worry that the coach won't start me in a meet the next day. I'm being torn in so many directions. The directors of each activity think their activity is the most important; they expect me to put their activity before anything else. They decide what days I do what. I hear the band director and the choir director fighting over me, or the choir director and the swimming coach arguing whenever there's a time conflict.

I don't quit anything I start. My mother says I have to drop something, but I refuse. I'm also on student government, in the art club, in the school musical every year, and on prom court for homecoming. Last year I had the musical, band, choir, I was taking an instrument, and I was on *two* swim teams. I quit the YMCA swim team toward the end of last season. I couldn't take it anymore.

Earlier this year I was so tired I thought I had mono, but I didn't. About four months ago I began to have violent stomachaches. The doctor tested me for all kinds of diseases, including your basic food allergies. He couldn't find a thing wrong with me.

I'm really feeling the pressure now. School swimming starts again soon, and I have to get my grades up for college. I would probably get much better grades—I get B's and would probably get A's—if I wasn't so involved in other things. I don't want swimming to start, but I feel obligated to be on the team. I like it a lot, but I am not looking forward to it. I've been swimming since I was seven; that's almost all I know.

I feel as if I have to do everything. I don't want to let my teammates down. I like winning. I think it's more difficult to lose once you are used to winning. It's not that I mind losing, it's what other people are saying and thinking—"I can't believe she lost. I never knew that Cindy Cornell would ever lose, ever not get a first place." You feel as if you are pleasing an audience in addition to pleasing yourself. How people react—the parents who are watching, the coach—is the hardest part of losing. People expect me to win.

I'm considering not swimming next year, but the team needs me. I don't mean to sound conceited, but I am good. *[In her freshman year Cindy broke—and still holds—the state's high-school records for both breaststroke and freestyle.]* If I get a lead role in the school musical it will be difficult to swim. Last year, with only a minor role, I got myself in trouble. I had to be at rehearsals at least two days a week and at swim practice the other days. But we have swim meets as often as three days a week, so I could never get to swim practice. There aren't enough days in my week. I wasn't in good shape.

If I'm in the play I'll dedicate myself to the play. I don't want to hurt my friends by not being in the play, because they will think I don't think the play is fun. The play is certainly more fun. Still, I can't let the team down; I owe it to them to swim this year. Once you start, you can't stop. It's almost like an obsession: you can't let yourself down; you can't let other people down. Whatever I quit, someone will be disappointed. I keep going so I don't disappoint anyone. I ask myself who am I doing this for. Me? The coach? Do I really like this, or am I doing it because this is what I've always done?

It's so hard to stop. If you stop one thing, a piece of you is missing. It's gone. Right now I'm in a nook and it's very hard to break away. It would be very weird. I don't think I would be the same to everyone else if I stopped. I'm torn and pulled in too many directions. The musical will be hard enough with choir and band and classes and my social life.

Swimming doesn't take the weekends, but band does. We have band competitions on Saturday nights and some Sundays, and we perform at the football games on Friday nights and often don't get home until one or two A.M. Plus I have to have some time to learn the music. I get jealous when I see my friends doing fun things on the weekend. (I have a lot of friends in the band, but it's not the same thing.) Today it's Sunday, and I have to sell cheesecakes for choir, Reese's Pieces and peanutbutter cups for the swim team, and raffle chances for the band. The neighbors are sick of me.

My friends are very demanding of my time, too. My mom always makes fun of me because I complain. I think I have more social life than anyone else in my school, because I have friends in different groups—swim-team friends, choir friends, band friends, drama friends. They all want their share of my time. No wonder I am tired. And when I'm stressed out, every little thing bothers me. I'm annoyed if a friend borrows a book and forgets to return it or someone says they will let me know what time a party starts and doesn't. Stupid little things, but they get to me because I'm overdoing everything.

I was nominated to homecoming court. You have to live up to that. You have to have a smile on your face the entire day or you lose votes. If you are in a bad mood, you don't get votes. I'm so glad elections are over. Now I can put my hair in a ponytail and wear sweats to school. I don't have to worry about how I look or whether or not I smile at everyone.

I've been talking to one of my mother's friends lately. She's been helping me see that I'm trying too hard. I'm getting better. When I'm annoyed I show it. I'm getting rid of my mask. I wake up and tell myself that I don't have to please the whole school every day. I don't have to be nice to everyone. I don't have to be involved in everything. I can decide to do things because *I* want to.

Postscript: A few weeks before swim practices began, Cindy had another painful stomach attack. This time her doctor considered doing an emergency appendectomy. Thinking the pains were caused by overexercising, Cindy decided to drop swimming. She proved to be her own best doctor. The coach called her up and "worked her over": "The team needs you. We can't win without you. You're letting the school down." But for Cindy, her health was more important.

She was given the starring role in the musical and now had time to enjoy rehearsals. Her stomach problems vanished. By simplifying her life, ever so slightly, she improved her health and, as she predicted, brought up her grades. The following year Cindy was accepted at three first-rate colleges, including her first choice.

FACTS TO FOCUS ON

■ Cindy Cornell is someone who can handle mountains of stress. She's been under fire since she was seven years old, with little ill effect. Cindy was a star in many arenas—too many, in fact. No one can handle all that Cindy piled on herself without suffering some negative reactions. Everyone has a breaking point.

■ We are each unique in how much and what kind of stress we can handle, and for how long. In Cindy's case her stress was created by overdoing it. Stress eventually catches up with most people. Your body will tell you when the stress is getting to be too great.

Physical problems created by stress tend to attack the body's most vulnerable systems. If it's the digestive system, for example, stress may cause stomachaches, constipation, or diarrhea. It may also produce a constant need to urinate.

■ Being outstanding—whether as a swimmer, musician, debater, soccer player, or cheerleader—can be a huge burden. People will count on you to give a peak performance every time. The feeling of being forced to perform in a certain way increases stress.

■ Sometimes stopping something is harder than continuing it. There's a real fear of losing friends and a sense of identity. Some teens also worry about how they will fill new-found free time.

■ Teenagers push themselves to excel for many reasons: to list lots of extracurricular activities on college applications, because their friends are participating, or to fit in.

■ Activity overload takes its toll on schoolwork too. As one high-school football quarterback says, "Football affected my grades. When I got home, I was too tired to pay much attention to my homework. I did what I could and went to sleep. It's coming back to haunt me now that it's time to go to college."

■ Stress to perform starts early. Many kindergarten children play team soccer, for example. If you started a sport, dance lessons, or music lessons 'way back in elementary school, you could be burned out by now. Just putting on a uniform or costume could send your stress level soaring.

■ The reverse is also true: you can feel stress from doing nothing. This is quite the opposite of what happened with Cindy, but it is stressful nonetheless. Not participating can be just as upsetting as being too involved.

■ Schools offer a wide variety of clubs and sports. There is something to interest everyone. You are not making a lifelong commitment when you sign up for the yearbook staff or the photography club. Y's and community centers have sports and unusual afterschool programs too. Call the local museum, if you have one nearby, to find out about their programs. Towns offer interesting courses and events. If you don't like the first thing you try, switch.

MOVING IN THE RIGHT DIRECTION

■ If the fun of an activity is gone, stop it or take some time off. Ask the coach or the activity's leader to allow you to miss a practice once a month or once a week. Skip a rehearsal now and then. If you are so important to the activity, your occasional absence will be tolerated. Be sure to clear your time off with the person in charge and explain why you are asking for it. Be straightforward: "I'm too strung out; I need a break," or "I'm bored." An honest explanation will be given serious consideration. After a break, the sport or pursuit may have a new appeal and hold new excitement.

■ Some parents are not as understanding as others. A displeased parent will eventually adjust to your decision. Give yours some time and they will come around.

■ When you take a break, use your free time to make yourself feel better. Don't worry about what you're not doing or feel you should be doing. Get exercise if you need it, or read a book if your body needs a rest. But avoid extended periods in front of the television. It can make you even more tired and fuzzy brained.

■ Those who want to do it all might consider spacing their activities out a bit to allow for a social life. Do only one winter sport or fall sport and combine it with a couple of clubs or perhaps the school newspaper. Figure out how much time each activity requires, then see if what is left over is enough for you.

■ Only now, when she is almost out of high school, is Cindy realizing that she needs time for herself. Free time is necessary for everyone to relax and think about what makes them happy. Making such choices about how to spend their time helps people develop a sense of who they are.

■ People who stop to analyze what they are doing and how it makes them feel are getting their lives in control. People who just keep going, loading themselves with responsibility without having fun, are emotionally out of control. In time, stressful feelings will take over. Stop to think about what you are doing and how it affects *you*.

■ Think, too, about why you are involved in many things, why you are overloaded—or why you work too hard and too many hours pursuing one goal. The key questions are: Are you, like Cindy, in a rut, doing something simply because it's what you have always done? Are your parents getting more pleasure from what you do than you are? Are you involved to please your friends, or yourself?

If the answer is honestly that you are involved for yourself, then stress is unlikely to be a problem. Do what you enjoy, but don't enjoy so many activities that they all bear down on you as they did for Cindy.

■ When you realize that you are a worthwhile person even if you do not overload your academic and extracurricular schedules, you will be able to find a suitable balance.

■ Be cautious not to get caught at the other extreme, however. If you don't get involved, people will not know your name or who you are. This is especially true if you attend a large school. Being involved in activities is a good way to improve your social life if it's less than what you want it to be.

■ By doing something—anything!—you avoid the stress of feeling left out, which can be as upsetting as being overcommitted.

2.

FIFTH-GRADE FLASHER

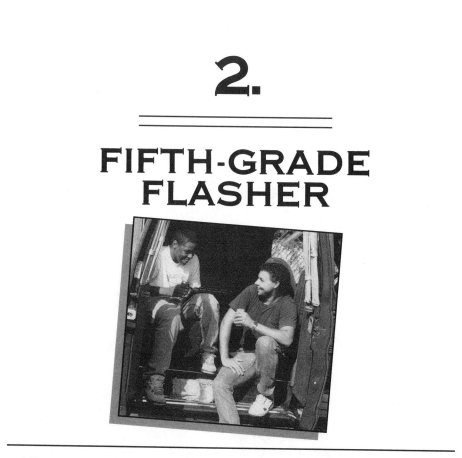

"I got off on the wrong track. Fooling around

in school worked for me. My parents were so

into education and insisting that I do well and

go to college. I don't know. It seemed

too hard. My mistake,"

admits Peter Henry, eighteen years old.

*T*he kids dared me. They offered me money. How could I refuse? They said I didn't have the nerve to flash the whole class. I did. My luck turned. As I approached the front of the room, my rear end exposed, the teacher walked in. That was the beginning of my troubles; my list is long and distinguished.

Flashing the fifth-grade class seemed to be the turning point for me. I never could get rid of that reputation. I was eleven, and marked for life. I was a conduct problem after that, which quickly led to me being an academic problem.

In grade school I didn't like the work. It's not that I couldn't do it; I didn't want to do it. I had plenty of hobbies that kept me from anything that had to do with my studies. My father would pull me

away from my model airplanes at night and stick me in a room after dinner with my books—no radio, no television. I couldn't study on command and, I thought, I couldn't concentrate without music or the television. I would sit and stare at the wall until he would let me out.

As I got older, instead of studying I spent hours in the park, throwing a football or shooting baskets. My parents were freaked out by my attitude and behavior. They are both well educated—my mother is a children's-book editor and my father is a biochemist. They kept telling me I was ruining my life. You know, the usual: how are you ever going to make anything of yourself? You can't earn a decent living if you don't go to college. That sort of thing. Constantly. My parents never let up on me.

Other kids who do poorly in school have problems at home—parents who abuse them or drink too much or get divorced. Me, I don't know; I wasn't a great student. I was a clown. Acting like a jerk seemed to work for me at the time, so I kept it up. The other kids laughed at me or with me, I'm not sure which, but I had tons of friends and was invited everywhere and to everything. I was good-time Pete, any time.

I was failing in high school from the day I got there. I started smoking pot when I was fifteen. Someone let me try it, I thought it was pretty good, so I bought a bag. My best friend and I would go into the fields and smoke. We smoked everywhere, including in front of school. It was part of my I-don't-care attitude.

I knew right from wrong. At that age I knew enough to make good choices. So I take responsibility. I can't blame my parents. You can't tell a fourteen- or fifteen-year-old to do something. They won't do it; they probably won't understand what you are talking about.

It didn't help the friction at home that my little brother was a super student. He was setting test-score records in the third grade in spite of my bad influence. He studied through my blasting radio and bouncing a basketball against the wall between our bedrooms. My parents' screaming must have frightened him into getting good grades. His being such a great student just made it harder. My parents thought that since we had the same genes we should both be smart.

I quit school when I was a senior. I knew it was a bad idea before I did it, but I didn't see a lot of alternatives. The principal had told me I was going to go on a five-year plan. In other words, I wasn't going to graduate with my class. I would need to go to school another year to get my credits. A fifth year of high school wasn't for me.

I thought about getting a GED [General Equivalency Degree], but that was a stupid idea. My friend Eric had tried that the year before. He got a GED and thought it was as good as a high-school diploma, but it isn't. You need the real thing, but neither one of us realized that. Eric called the Air Force, the Army, and the Marines. You can't get in with only a GED anymore; you need fifteen college credits, too.

Eric will be stuck doing road work for the rest of his life. He's tough, but it wears him out. He has a lot of energy, but he's tired at the end of the day. He doesn't even like what he's doing. He jokes about it, but I know he's real unhappy. I suppose if he were doing something he enjoyed, or he wasn't forced to do what the foreman tells him, he might like it better. When he quit school he closed out a lot of his choices.

When you are out of school for a month or so, you're doing nothing, or in my case drinking and smoking pot, you realize you've blown it. My parents were furious. They have had it with me. They gave up. They were tired of talking to teachers and guidance counselors to try to straighten me out. They did it for years. Everyone needs to make his own mistakes, but if you can avoid the big ones, like dropping out of school, you'll be way ahead.

I had to grow up really fast as soon as I dropped out of school. My parents cut me off when I quit. That's when I realized how hard it is to

make it in today's world. I had to take part-time jobs at fast-food places, the car wash, and at the supermarket bagging groceries. Like Eric, I was tired and short of money all the time.

I would have loved to be going to college with my friends and teammates. I had it made, too. I didn't need especially good grades, because I was a star forward—high scorer every game. I would have gotten a full scholarship with just passing grades. I've got determination and drive and I'm aware of it. I'm through screwing up my life. I got sidetracked, that's all. I was in drug rehabilitation for six months to stop smoking marijuana. I couldn't get off the stuff by myself.

After rehab I decided to try high school again. The credit belongs to my basketball coach. He's the one who put the idea in my head. He told me I could have my starting spot on the team if I kept my grades up. I took school seriously for the first time since fifth grade. I got A's in several of my classes. I realized I was pretty smart—not as smart as my little brother, but smart enough.

Looking at my high-school record you can see the turnaround. I'm wiser now, more reasonable. Logical thinking has taken over . . . finally. I have discipline; I've grown up.

I'm starting college in the fall on a partial basketball scholarship. If I hadn't fooled around, I probably could have gotten a full scholarship at a bigger college, maybe one of the big universities. With my academic record, they're taking a chance on me, but they won't be sorry.

FACTS TO FOCUS ON

- Peter Henry came from an academically oriented family. He couldn't live up to his parents' standards. A teenager with parents or siblings who are successful in school or in their careers may feel intense pressure to do well. For Peter, the stress was too much.

- Parents who were academically unsuccessful may also push too hard. They may want more for their children than they had. The reverse may also be true: parents who did not finish high school may feel that their children don't have to complete high school either. But in today's world it is unrealistic to believe that you can be an outstanding success without having at least a high-school education.

- Parents who push their children often end up with teenagers who rebel, as Peter did. Likewise, parents who offer academic advice are more apt to have teens who follow it. The stress is less for those who make their own decision to do well.

- To escape stress, Peter became the class clown, then turned to drugs. Drug use made his personal life more complicated and his chance for school success impossible.

- In overcrowded schools, many students go nameless and are not noticed unless they excel scholastically or, like Pete, become troublemakers.

■ When a student becomes disruptive or does poorly in his studies, as Peter did, the school psychologist is often asked to do an evaluation. This helps determine what may be causing the difficulties and what type of help a student needs. Evaluations can pinpoint special problems called learning disabilities. Once the problems are discovered, the school can adjust the work so it's less of a strain, or give the student special instruction to deal with a learning problem.

■ Being in a highly competitive academic environment can be as distressing as not getting good grades. To be compared with brilliant students when you may not be quite as bright can be discouraging and nerve-wracking. Such a situation is especially stressful when parents don't understand the pressure.

■ Long hours at part-time jobs eat into study time. Bosses don't think twice about asking for an extra hour of work here and there, especially if you are a conscientious worker. The hours and the dollars add up, but studies quickly fall behind and tension mounts.

■ Changing schools can create stress and affect a student's work. The switch can be a regular move from junior high to high school. But a move into a different school system can have an even greater effect. In a new school there will be concern over how well other students are doing. In the old, familiar school, the academic competition was known. Within a few weeks, however, a new student will understand the abilities of his peers.

■ Even students who live in neighborhoods surrounded by crack dens and drug dealers, with schools protected by metal detectors and guards, *have* succeeded. In these surroundings it may seem as if getting into college—not to mention getting out of high school—is hopeless. Students in these situations who want to learn must make an extra effort to let their teachers know that they are serious.

■ No matter what school they attend, few people succeed without applying themselves. Jim Cullin is a case in point: "Freshman and sophomore year I laid back and didn't think about college. Then—pow—S.A.T.'s crept up on me. I worried about my grades. I felt as if every test was going to affect the rest of my life. I'm not going to get a good grade on this test, which means I'm not going to get a good grade in the course, which means I'm not going to get into college. I'd get myself so worked up that I couldn't go to sleep at night.''

■ Even with an outstanding high-school record, the process of getting admitted to college is a major source of stress.

MOVING IN THE RIGHT DIRECTION

■ Because you're maturing, your mind will be occupied with more than one important thing at a time. Part of being mature is being able to perform well without being distracted when you have several things to accomplish.

■ Although some students perform better under stress than others, most do their best by removing as many sources of stress as possible. You cannot get rid of your big sister, but you can avoid a friend who would rather smoke pot than attend class. You may not be able to get A's on every quiz, but you will do better by studying than by going into a test without cracking a book.

If the work is too difficult, talk to your guidance counselor. Perhaps you can be moved into a less stressful group that is more matched to your abilities.

■ If life at home is unpleasant, you may have trouble concentrating. Pack your books and do your assignments at the library, the local Y, or at a friend's house. Completing your assignments will eliminate that gnawing feeling of undone work hanging over your head.

■ The organized person and the person who has decided in advance to work hard will experience less stress related to school pressures. Students who are prepared for class and ready for tests are less likely to feel stressed.

■ Organized people accomplish more—both more easily and more quickly. Use an assignment book, and get missed lessons from friends or directly from the teacher. Block out the time you need to study. Then stick to the schedule you have set.

Don't let your mind wander. And don't interrupt your studying to make a quick phone call or have a snack. Save the phone calls and food as rewards for completing an assignment or finishing a review for a test.

- Study periods work best when they run an hour or two, depending on your span of concentration, followed by a break of fifteen to thirty minutes. Exercise during the break. A fifteen-minute walk, bike ride, or jog will improve your mood. The oxygen you breathe in while exercising will help clear your head for studying.

- A student should keep reminding himself that he is an individual person doing the best he can do. Don't feel down if you are not meeting your parents' expectations. They may want more from you than you are capable of producing.

- However, having a poor record as a result of being lazy may not be worth the loss of self-esteem. Run yourself through the paces for one marking period: do your assignments and be well prepared for class. You may discover that you are a happier person when the next report card arrives.

- There is usually a specific reason for a noticeable downward turn in a teenager's school performance. There may be problems at home, arguments with parents, divorcing parents, illness, or being abandoned by a friend. Any personal upset can be reflected—usually temporarily—in a student's schoolwork without his realizing it.

- You're moving in the right direction if you figure out what is causing you to ignore your school responsibilities and then give your education your best shot.

3.

NO TIME TO BE A KID

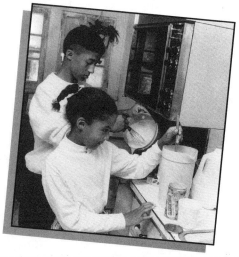

"I want to get married someday, but my parents' divorce makes me think that maybe I'll pick the wrong person. I don't want my children to live through what I've had to live through."

Frank Remez says he will get his life together before he considers marriage and children.

I remember the first time I was told. My little sister Lisa cried and cried. I tried to cheer her up. I was thirteen years old. My mother said that Dad was moving out. I thought, this is great. There was so much tension in our family. I thought that without my father our lives would be calmer.

Their making it official didn't have too much effect on me, because I was already affected by the years of fighting. The arguments between my parents were pretty bad. They were usually in the evening, because my father didn't get home from work until after nine

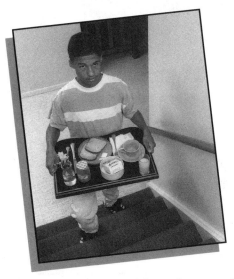

o'clock, sometimes much later. When he got home he wanted everything waiting and perfect. He wanted my sister and me quiet; dinner, warm and delicious. If it wasn't, I knew there would be trouble. He was mad most of the time. He has a bad temper.

At night in bed I listened to angry yelling and screaming. It hurt me, because my mother and I are very close. My father was much bigger than I was then. There was not too much I could do, but I wanted to protect my mother. I just didn't know how. It seemed so unfair. I felt powerless. I lay in my bed sweating, with a pillow over my head to drown out their words.

If Lisa and I happened to be around, they put a lot of pressure on us, asking us who was right and who was wrong. Often I gave my father a hard time, but it was useless. I asked him why he kept yelling at my mother. My sister didn't say much to him or give him any kind of an argument. I felt helpless. I couldn't seem to do anything to stop my father from being mean or to make my mother happy.

One Sunday morning I decided to give Mom breakfast in bed. My father told me not to, but I did it anyway. I figured he would respect me for doing such a nice thing. He didn't. He yelled and yelled at me. It took me years to realize he acted that way because he felt guilty. He didn't know how to handle his guilt except to lash out at my mother and me.

My parents went to meetings and parties together. People never knew that they didn't get along, but ever since I can remember they fought. I think they stayed together for convenience and to keep up appearances. No one knew from me, either, that there was anything going on at home. I smiled through everything; it looked as if I had a perfect life. I thought that I shouldn't let the turmoil at home carry over into my life away from home. I thought I didn't need to talk, but everyone does. The parts of your life are related, and one part affects the others.

I longed for a normal family. My best friend has this big, happy family. There are six kids, and the parents and kids get along very well. I can talk to him about anything in the world except my parents' ugly marriage. He could never understand the fighting in our house. I would have died to have a warm family like his. I thought about that all the time. I wanted a father who was married to my mother forever, to come home and see my real parents, the ones who had me, being happy. I imagined that had to be the best feeling.

I couldn't do my schoolwork, couldn't concentrate on anything other than making my parents love each other. I was the one always trying to make things better, to straighten things out between my mother and father. I would go back and forth between them, telling one that the other one really loved him or her and that everything would be okay.

It never occurred to me that divorce was a possibility. I didn't think about that. I was simply trying to make peace and keep everyone happy. I tried talking to my parents one on one. I was young—thirteen. It's too much for a kid. I never really had the time to be a kid.

I felt as if I never did enough. I was constantly going and doing, but no one ever told me I was doing a good job. Neither parent noticed when I washed the car, stacked the wood, started dinner, or helped Lisa with her homework. I stopped being a good guy and started doing pretty much whatever I felt like doing—going to school when I wanted, leaving when I wanted, doing homework when I felt like it, going out at night and coming home late—but not caring. I did a lot worse the year of the divorce than I ever had before. I had so many absences I had to go to summer school.

Making up school was the easy part. I was nervous and afraid much of the time, and went to the bathroom in my pants regularly, especially when my father was home. When I slept, I went into such a deep sleep that I wet the bed until I was fifteen. I couldn't stop. After my father left, I finally got myself under control.

In the beginning I was happy that Dad left, but I had so much more responsibility than my friends. My mother went back to school. The list of chores I had to do got much longer. I had to take care of Lisa full time, do the lawn, clean the house, and make dinner.

I didn't love my father then. My dislike for him grew when I found out that he had been seeing other women while he was still married to my mother. The worst part was that my father is a respected member of the community. He's a doctor, the head of the largest hospital in this area. He's also well known for a treatment for kidney infections that he discovered before he gave up research and took this hospital job. Yet the big do-gooder who saves lives was so nasty to Lisa, to me, and to my mother.

For the first four years he was out of the house I refused to talk to him. I started stealing, smoking cigarettes, and using most kinds of drugs. The drugs caught up with me quickly. When I stopped using them, even for a day or so, the withdrawal symptoms were horrible. I was irritable and lost my appetite. I wasn't able to sleep. Then I realized that I needed the drugs, that they were really addictive. I saw that if I didn't stop then, I was never going to stop. It was scary.

I didn't have anything to do with my father during my drug years. My mother knew, but she couldn't stop me. She was busy at work and trying to finish her master's degree so that she could land a higher-paying job.

I take responsibility for my actions since the divorce, and even before. I used poor judgment, but now I'm able to make good choices for myself.

My father has changed, too. Like me, he's a person, and everyone makes mistakes. He isn't able to tell me that he's sorry or that what he did was wrong. I love him anyway.

Lisa still has trouble not having my father around, but my mother is happy. My mother feels that my father is trying to win my sister over. He buys her presents and takes her away on fancy trips with him. At least he can admit to Lisa that he does these things because he feels bad about leaving. He knows he can't buy me.

To this day, my parents talk about each other. They have both remarried, but after I visit my father my mother questions me about

him. And while I'm visiting my Dad he pumps for information about my mother. I never tell him anything, because if I happen to mention that my mother and I have disagreed about something he will jump on it and tell me it will only get worse. "That's just like your mother. You'll see." I can't take his word about her, or hers about him. I make up my own mind about the two of them.

Marriage scares me. I'm afraid that I'm not going to be able to have a good marriage, because I haven't seen one in my own family. I don't understand how you can love someone for fifteen years and then stop. I know it happens all the time, but I don't want it to happen to me.

FACTS TO FOCUS ON

■ During your lifetime there has been an enormous increase in the divorce rate. Half of all marriages today end in divorce. This means that one out of two children live with, or have lived part of their growing years with, only one parent.

■ Some parents are very private about the problems between them. They keep to themselves and do not involve their children. Others, unfortunately, put their children in the middle of every disagreement and use them as messengers. Involving young children and teenagers like this creates added stress. It is not a teenager's job, for example, to be sure that a child-support check arrives.

■ Adults involved in a divorce ask a lot of their teenage children. These teenagers are asked to be independent, to take charge quite early in life. But then they see their world falling apart around them. This is enough to fill teens with despair and have them ask, as Frank Remez did, "Why work so hard at relationships, at life?"

■ After a separation or divorce, there may be a drastic change in lifestyle. The family income is divided to support two households. A previously nonworking parent may go to work to increase the family's income. The family may be forced to move. Parents as well as children must live with insecurity and adjust to changes.

■ Some teens find that they have become in effect a parent to one of their own parents. They may become too protective. When they see the loss, they may rush to fill in for the parent who has moved out, just as Frank did. Not only will they comfort the distressed parent emotionally, but they may also be asked to take over for the absent parent around the house, doing chores and caring for younger siblings. Such extra burdens add to the normal stress of breaking up a family.

■ It is not uncommon for a parent to be hard on a child who resembles or has the habits and mannerisms of the other parent. Ricky Stand, who was twelve when his parents divorced, knows well how this can happen. "Instead of my Dad, my mother started picking on me, yelling at me something fierce. I suppose that's because he and I look so much alike. Looking at me was like looking at him."

■ The friction of divorce can go on for years. "The conflicts between my parents have been going on since the divorce. That was five years ago,"explains sixteen-year-old Helena Yung. "My mother has been trying to get my dad to give us more money. She's going to take him to court again soon." Helena holds up fingers to indicate that this will be the fourth court visit.

■ Many teens respond to divorce by doing poorly in school. This temporary lapse occurs while the transitions created by the divorce are being made. Usually their grades bounce back once the crisis is over and they can concentrate again.

■ Just because adults are messing up doesn't mean their teenagers should do the same. Frank Remez made the mistake of turning to drugs, thinking they would soften the blows of a problem that wasn't even his.

MOVING IN THE RIGHT DIRECTION

■ Teenagers who believe that they have had nothing to do with their parents' difficulties are better able to handle the stress of their parents' separation or divorce than those who feel they contributed to it.

■ It's best not to interfere. There is probably no way children can keep parents from arguing. When your parents fight, get away from them. Head for your room, over to a friend's house, or out for a walk.

■ If you have to move and change schools because of a separation or divorce, you will probably be angry. Concentrate instead on what could be positive outcomes: making new friends, eating out more often, and having less tension in the house. By examining the potential pluses of the divorce you can find things to look forward to.

■ Those who cannot find anything good after the "dust has settled" would be wise to seek counseling to help them sort out their confusion and unhappiness. Your own happiness is still attainable, even though your parents could not find it in their marriage.

■ During the tough times you need someone to tell you that you're doing fine. Suzanne Ossing, who is seventeen, offers this advice: "Don't keep everything inside. I got to the point where I was sitting in school crying. Every little thing set me off. So I confided in a teacher I like and in my guidance counselor."

■ Be prepared for one or both parents to do things that you think are off the wall or are less than considerate of you or your feelings. Parents who are dating sometimes act younger than their teenage children. When one parent announces plans to remarry, the other parent may resort to crazy measures to try to prevent the remarriage. Some adults can never accept the fact that their spouse has left them.

■ When your parents are a disappointment to you, your feelings of being connected to others will pull you through periods of despair. The connection may be to a counselor, a friend, or a friend's parent. Christopher Spence couldn't talk to his closest friends about his parents' divorce so as he says, "I found a new friend whose family was in the middle of the same kind of mess mine was. We talked; we were good for each other."

PART II

DON'T BE ANXIOUS

*I*t's usually possible to figure out what causes stress, because the stressor is frequently related to an event or a specific condition. We have seen that Cindy Cornell had too many commitments, Peter Henry messed up in school, and Frank Remez weakened amidst the double turmoil of his father's toughness and his parents' divorce. Anxiety is different from stress, however. Anxiety stems from something internal. It's a vague, undefined fear—of some unknown danger or calamity. Sometimes anxiety starts out as stress. In other words, anxiety is very often stress that is left unresolved. People under stress can be anxious; that is, they can be fearful, but without knowing exactly why.

There is no one clearly defined form for stress or anxiety. Either condition depends both on who you are and what the situation is. One fourteen-year-old whose mother is an alcoholic explains her confusion, "I don't rush home from school. Why should I? But there is a side of me that wants to rush home. I want to be there long enough to make sure my mother hasn't started a fire on the stove and burned down the house, or left the gas on in the oven and passed out on the couch with the windows closed." This teenager's conflict about her mother keeps her in an almost constant state of anxiety. She's under stress to protect her mother and she is afraid that something will happen to her.

The pressure to be sexually active can also create unexplained feelings of uneasiness, confusion, and anxiety. If you watch television for even the shortest amount of time, life will begin to look sexy. Television shows build themes around sex. Commercials scream at you that if you buy their product you'll be a sexier person and catch your man or woman. What you see on television is designed either to sell products or to entertain.

In the real world, having intercourse does not make you feel more grown up, unlike the way it is shown in the make-believe world of movies and television. It will not make you feel sexier, because sex is a mental experience as much as a physical one. Teenage sexual relationships are for the most part, purely physical ones, not emotional and not mature.

A person who is anxious about having intercourse is frightened that she will not be able to cope with a situation, that she will mess up or meet with bad luck. The teenager who was afraid that her mother would burn down the house or die faced the same situation every day. This situation was out of her control. When you don't know what you can do or feel that you have no options, stress and anxiety increase.

When you see that there are choices, stress and anxiety become less intense. By making the decision to refuse to drink or to stay away from the situations that could provide the opportunity for intimate sex, you can eliminate much of the nervousness and uncertainty that cause anxiety.

Teenagers are much better equipped to cope with anxiety when they have a good idea of who they are. People who have defined themselves well will be more likely to be able to withstand pressure to drink at parties or to become sexually involved before they are ready to be.

Strong, uneasy feelings of anxiety can be caused by difficult conditions, such as living with a parent who abuses you. They can also be caused by situations that change your life, such as being arrested by the police or becoming pregnant before you are mature enough to be a mother. The responsibility of protecting and caring for a small child makes even many older parents anxious.

A panic attack is very different from high anxiety. Any teenager would recognize such an attack as being more than the usual nervousness. It's a terrible experience, and people talk about a panic attack as if it was the worst event of their lives. In a panic attack you think your heart is going to burst out of your chest; you think you are going to faint; you become so dizzy you think you are going to fall down. Some people become short of breath or start choking during a panic attack. Others think they are going to die or go crazy. These states are not normal. It is unusual for teenagers to have panic attacks. According to those who have spent years studying such attacks, most people who have them don't do so until they are in their mid-twenties. If you think you are having panic attacks, tell someone. It is much easier to control them or eliminate them when they are just beginning, before they have a chance to establish themselves.

Most of us experience anxiety in a much less terrifying way. Suppose, for instance, that you have to give an oral report in English class. The mere idea makes your hands perspire. Some people don't like to speak in front of groups, even small ones. Others do not like going into new and unfamiliar surroundings. Under such conditions anxiety can take over. Intense feelings of fear then command you, and you are unable to command the situation. People handle anxiety in their own ways. Some refuse to face the situation or, if they do, are extremely shy. Others get shaky. Still others get physically ill with stomachaches or headaches.

Here's a list of things you can do in situations that make you nervous or frightened. If you work at these suggestions you will be able to face everyday events in your life more calmly.

1. Practice whatever you have to do. If it's a speech, go over it many times. If it's trying out for a sport, play as often as you can. With a new dance, learn the steps in advance.
2. Bear in mind that there will almost always be someone who is better, but also someone who is lots worse, than you are.
3. Pat yourself on the back each time you do something great. Don't dwell on your weaknesses. Keep reminding yourself that you can do whatever you set your mind to doing. Eventually you will believe it.
4. When you see a friend or an adult acting the way you would like to—taking charge or handling a difficult situation with ease—copy as much of that person's behavior as possible.
5. Ask a friend if he or she ever felt the way you do. You may be surprised to learn that lots of other people are overwhelmed by the same problems that affect you.

The circumstances in the stories that follow are far more complex and anxiety producing than starring in a play, being outgoing on a date, or giving a report in class. In order to cope with anxiety the people in these stories had to find new avenues to pursue and new outlets to make their lives manageable. In short, change—drastic change—is often necessary in order to reduce anxiety or remove oneself from anxiety-ridden situations.

4.

CINDERELLA'S STEPMOTHER

"When my father came home she started again.

'Maybe I should shove the key down your throat

to make you remember where it is.' She slapped

me. My father watched and said nothing,"

recalls Melissa Field,

now twenty-two years old.

*M*y mother left home, disappeared for good, when I was two years old. My father and I moved in with his parents. While we lived with them I had a wonderful, happy life.

I walked home from school. My grandmother was always so glad to see me. She helped me with my homework and made sure my clothes were neat. I had bows in my hair and sometimes she curled it. As a special treat she polished my toenails bright red. We baked cookies every Saturday, and whenever we made a cake I got to lick the bowl and the beaters.

When I was in fourth grade my father remarried. I lived the next nine years in what I quickly came to view as prison. Angela, my

father's wife, was my prison guard. Even though I didn't know my real mother, I could never bring myself to call Angela "Mom." I was too afraid of her.

From the very start of life in our new house, I had adult chores. I was responsible for making the coffee in the morning, setting out the cups for my father and Angela, getting my own breakfast, making my lunch, and waking them for work. My new school was more than a mile away. I walked alone both ways until I made friends.

The first day I came home from school I was terrified. I jumped every time the wind blew the curtains or made the house creak. I was afraid to move off the chair at the kitchen table. I called my grandmother just to make me feel better, but she came over immediately to keep me company. When Angela got home from work she threw a fit. As soon as my grandmother left she shouted, "How dare you call your grandmother? Who do you think you are? Go to your room. Go to bed. No dinner." My father listened, but he never said a word.

One Christmas, before going to dinner at my aunt's house, I fed the cat and put her downstairs. I hadn't checked the milk. When Angela discovered that the milk was turning sour—the milk would not have harmed the cat—she smacked me across the face and pushed me over to the open basement door. "Now you go look at that milk!" she screamed, and shoved me down the steps. I didn't think about being hurt. As I rolled I just waited to reach the bottom. My ears rang for four days. When I complained, Angela said, "It's your own fault."

My assignments around the house increased steadily. Angela didn't ever help; she watched and criticized. By fifth grade I had to wash the breakfast dishes, make dinner, change the beds, clean the house. The house was never clean enough for Angela. I had to scrub the baseboards once a month. I often felt like Cinderella, but I wasn't old enough for Prince Charming.

If I breathed wrong, I was in trouble. So when I lost my house key I was scared to death of what she would do to me. The steps again, but different ones. This time no carpeting. Two banks of cement steps led from our front door to the sidewalk. She pushed me down the first set, came running after me, pulled my face up to hers by my hair, and spit in it. She often spit at me while screaming "I don't want to see you again! The sight of you sickens me; I'm taking you to an orphanage. Your grandparents are too good for you." Then she spat on me and threw me down the second set of steps.

Angela came from a very poor family. She was very into upstaging the Joneses. When I was a freshman in high school Angela and my dad adopted a baby. Angela stopped working, which along with having the big house represented a step up for her. But the novelty of an infant wore off quickly. Getting the baby up, feeding him, bathing him, dressing him so that he was ready when Angela decided to have coffee were added to my before-school job list.

In addition to having to cook dinner every night, I had to make Angela and my father two drinks. I figured out at twelve that if I had to do the housework, care for my stepbrother, and make their drinks, I might as well make myself a drink, too. That's how my alcoholism developed. When I went to dances I took a little of this, a little of that from the liquor cabinet, put it in a jar and carried it out under my coat to the dance. As I got older, I matched Angela and my father drink for drink.

As soon as I started going out with friends on weekend evenings, Angela's slapping increased. If I was ten or fifteen minutes late, there was one punch for each minute. She hurled her arm and hit me with a clinched fist—always the back of her hand with her fingers squeezed tightly together. I had fat lips and black eyes regularly, but no adult ever asked me about them. Most of the time my girlfriends shook their heads and couldn't believe that Angela was beating me so much. I used to die to sleep over at a girlfriend's house, so I wouldn't have to face Angela.

My friends and I had a meeting place at the mall. I went to the mall with my friends one night and Angela found out. I was told I looked like a whore hanging out waiting for boys. That time she hit me with a bedroom slipper. Always on the face and arms. The slipper became a regular part of Angela's beating ritual.

At fifteen I had had enough. I left home. I took the train to New York with forty dollars in my pocket. Angela couldn't stand the fact that I had walked out. She couldn't face admitting to her friends that her daughter had run away. How would that look? She hired a private investigator to find me.

In front of Grand Central Station I asked two young girls where I could spend the night. They invited me home. I was lucky. I'm not sure what would have happened to me if their mother had not taken me in. A week later, I called my old boyfriend and he convinced me to return. His mother said that I could live with them.

The private investigator was on the platform to meet my train. That was one beating I will never forget. Angela had saved up a week's worth of rage. She called me a slut, a tramp, and a whore. She spat, she shook me, she slammed her fist in my face, but I was years beyond crying. I had built up my defenses to the point that I could stand there and say to myself, "Go ahead, beat me to death. I don't care. You want a tear. Sorry, lady, you can't have everything you want."

One day shortly after I had come back from New York Angela caught me smoking. She waited until my father got home before she started slamming me around. "You want to smoke?" she shrieked. "Here's a full pack of cigarettes. Eat it." She made me eat every one of them. I was never so sick in my whole life. That time I would rather have gotten beaten.

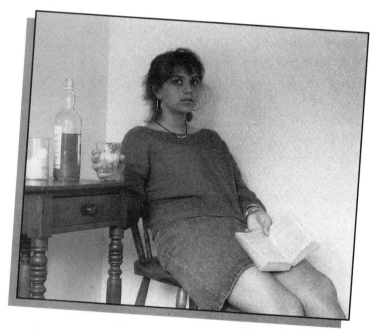

During my senior year of high school I got tired of being Angela's housekeeper and of never knowing when my next beating was coming or for what stupid reason. I packed my clothes and found a room and a job a few towns away. I drank alone in my room. The two drinks before dinner had become five or six or more until I lost track over the course of an evening.

After all these years, Angela still felt it wasn't good for her image to have one of her children leave home. An investigator found me three months later. My father called and asked me to come home and finish high school. That was one of the few times my father said anything to me. He usually sat on the couch and watched Angela beat me.

I never mentioned Angela to my father. If he could allow her to hit me, whose side was he on? I could see no point in asking him for help. There was constant silence on my father's part. If we were alone in the car, we didn't speak. The radio filled the car with sound.

At school I was judged the bad girl who had run away. To the school's officials my parents were giving me so much but in return I gave them trouble. I was ungrateful. I had lost three months of my senior year, and the school refused to give me my diploma unless I attended summer school. I found a job that allowed me to go to summer school, so I agreed to live at home until I had finished. I stayed away from Angela. My father, it appeared, had the same idea. He had gotten into a pattern of working late, not getting home until after ten, often after eleven.

One evening I was in my room on the telephone. Angela must have heard me laughing, because she picked up the extension in her bedroom and shrieked, "Get in here this instant!" I don't know what set her off, maybe my laughing, or the idea that I might be having fun. She started punching me. She grabbed my hair, which was very long at the time, and narrowed her eyes. "You know," she said, "you and this hair have got to go." She grabbed a pair of scissors and pulled my hair up to the top of my head, ready to snip. She was going to cut off my hair—all of it. Just then my father walked in and yelled "Stop!"

"Whose side are you on, anyway?" Angela yelled back. "How are you supposed to raise this child, who runs away, stops going to school, and does whatever she pleases?"

The next morning I went to New York City again, and never returned to that house. I saw my father and Angela at my grandfather's funeral. My grandmother told me to come to her house. "You don't have to be in the same room with Angela." My grandmother must have known something was not right, but she probably could never put her finger on exactly what it was, and I never told her. Maybe I should have.

When I moved to New York, I became an escort. I hated what I was doing, but the money was good. I became heavily involved with drugs—cocaine, heroin, snorting it at first, then mainlining—to forget what I was doing.

I left New York before I needed detoxing from heroin, but my drinking progressed. I do my drinking at home and by myself, not in bars or at parties. Even I can see that my drinking is out of control.

FACTS TO FOCUS ON

■ Anyone living with a parent who abuses her as Melissa Field's stepmother did must try to get out of that living arrangement before lifelong damage is done. Melissa's use of alcohol and heavy drugs, as well as her turning to prostitution, never had to happen. Had she told her grandmother or a counselor at school, her life might have been very different. By exposing her stepmother, Melissa might well have saved herself years of anxiety and of being brutally abused. The results of telling cannot be worse than what comes out of so much abuse.

■ For a long time, Melissa never realized that her home life was strange. Abused teenagers often don't know that other parents treat their children kindly, because they have never seen it in their own homes. It is not normal to have a parent who belittles you or makes you feel worthless. And it is not normal to have a parent who hits you regularly. Nor is it normal, or healthy, to have a parent who terrifies you.

■ Many parents who abuse their children physically or verbally are on drugs or are addicted to alcohol. "I'll never forgive my father," says Chet Kurplank. "Whenever he got drunk—pretty often before I ran away, he beat me with a boat oar over and over, as far back as I can remember. I don't know what he was trying to prove."

■ The emotional abuse that Melissa endured can be just as damaging to a person's well-being as physical abuse. Leah Messeli, age sixteen, took charge of her alcoholic father and the house after her mother walked out and feels that nothing she does is good enough. "In the mornings my father is so sweet and nice; we sit and have coffee and talk; by the end of the day he makes me feel awful. He yells and calls me names, tells me that I'm selfish and immature and irresponsible, and thinks everything I do is insignificant."

■ If a parent tells a child for long enough that she is no good, she begins to believe it. The combination of anxiety about what the parent will say or do and the actual physical harm that is done by some abusive parents often leads the abused person—Melissa in this case—to resort to drugs, promiscuity, and even suicide.

■ There are more than 20,000 agencies throughout the country that can advise and assist teens with their family problems. But there are only about 500 youth shelters for the half-million to a million teens who cannot live at home because their parents are abusive to them. Overcrowded and lacking space, these shelters have to turn away thousands of teenagers who need their services. These teens are left to fend for themselves on the streets.

MOVING IN THE RIGHT DIRECTION

■ Running away with no place to go can be as unpleasant as staying home with an abusive parent, stepparent, aunt, or uncle. If things are unbearable at home, a relative should be the next step. If no relatives are available, a foster home is one option but the streets are not. The streets are dangerous. They are homes for pimps, molesters, and drug dealers who won't think twice about taking advantage of you. Before you abandon home, think carefully about where you will sleep and how you will live.

■ Set up temporary escape plans in case you need them. Make a list of safe places you can go: a relative's house, a friend's house, the Y, or a community center. Keep the police telephone number handy, or memorize it.

■ Don't be embarrassed to ask for help. If you cannot get help from a school counselor or one of the social-service agencies listed in the front of your telephone book, call one of the national hotlines, most of which have people who can answer your questions twenty-four hours a day.

Covenant House provides advice and emergency help; its number is (800) 999-9999. Also available nationwide are the Runaway Switchboard (800) 621-4000 and the Runaway Hotline (800) 231-6946. Phone numbers for various Crisis Intervention Services and Child Abuse Control agencies are listed in the front of most telephone books under headings like Family and Children's Services.

■ It's never too late to change the course of your life. However, nothing will happen unless you take action. You have to care enough about yourself to make a telephone call or tell someone about the problem.

■ Temporary housing is possible at a host family when it is impossible to stay at home. Host families are available through a crisis intervention counselor at your school or through the intervention unit at the local hospital. In extreme cases such as Melissa's, if her grandmother had been unable to take her in Melissa could have lived with a host family for a few weeks, then be permanently placed in a youth shelter or foster care.

■ Host families can also be a solution when a cooling-down period is necessary between teens and parents. A teen who is having raging arguments with her parents might be put into a host family overnight or for a few days until the family can attend counseling sessions. The parent abuser is not told where the teenager is living, whether it's a temporary or a permanent arrangement.

■ A wise fifteen-year-old, Michael Waters, warns those who are being abused. "I know that children who grow up with an abusing parent very frequently become abusing parents themselves. I'm going to be very careful. I have a short fuse, but I'm aware and I'm going to keep my temper in control."

■ Parents who abuse teens will place the blame wherever they can. But, as in divorce, it is not the child's fault, no matter what that teenager has done. You need to accept the fact that there are some things you don't know and won't be able to know about why adults abuse their children. They often don't know the reasons themselves.

5.

DECISION MAKER

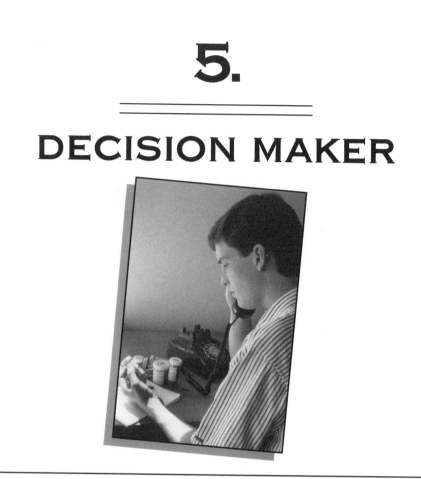

"My mom's situation was an example to my friends. Many of them have stopped using drugs. Like me, they decided it's not worth the hassle," confides solemn fifteen-year-old Judd Lawrence.

*M*y mother was recently cured of a drug problem she had had since she was eighteen. She was in a methadone clinic when I was very young, but she continued to use methadone and Valium and smoke pot until recently.

She says she wasn't doing drugs while she was pregnant with me, but I'm not so sure I believe her. I was underweight at birth and premature, which are both signs of drug use during pregnancy. She's not known for telling the truth.

My mother and I live with my dad, then we don't. (That is, if he is my dad. With my mother, who knows?) He comes and goes pretty much as he pleases. He supports us financially, but leaves whenever the going gets tough.

Before this last hospitalization, when Dad wasn't around, being with my mother was murder. She would say one thing and ten minutes later say something else. I started to think I was going crazy. My mother would tell me who I could be friendly with and what I could do. I can't play football, because she's afraid that I'll get hurt. She made me cut my hair every two weeks, so I looked as if I was in the Air Force. I felt as if I had no say in anything.

My friends are afraid of her, and those who aren't tell their parents about her bizarre behavior. Their parents forbid them to come to my house. At school they used to act as if I was a stranger. I began hanging out with other people who were more like my mother. My crowd became a very down crowd, a drug crowd.

I began to think: I know a lot of people who smoke pot and say it's no big deal. My mother is a smart person; Dad is a successful film producer. He has access to every drug imaginable, although he's not addicted. Whenever I questioned my mother, even when I was eight or nine years old, she insisted that marijuana was not a drug. I figured that if both my parents were using marijuana it must be okay. There were many occasions when I racked my brain—should I try it? Should I try it?

I tried it. I was so upset. I looked in the mirror and saw a male version of my mom. If that's what happens, I'm finished. I told my mother I had smoked, but she hardly reacted. I blew up. "You're a mother. You're not supposed to allow me to do these things." I couldn't be a hypocrite telling my mother to stop and then go out with friends and smoke dope.

If my mother used drugs during pregnancy, I'm prone to becoming addicted. My grandmother, grandfather, and uncle are alcoholics and my mother is a drug addict.

Drugs are a waste of time. I've seen that firsthand. Some of the time Mom was so wired she didn't know what she was doing; other times she couldn't be budged. Once she took Dad's car, put it in neutral, and let it roll down the steep hill in front of our house. It crashed into a tree and was totaled.

At times Mom got violent. If she couldn't reach me, she would break dishes and chairs, whatever was in her hand. I'm much bigger than she is. I could stop her and hold her, but she is my mother. It doesn't seem right to hold down your own mother.

I hated being home more than anything. I began to stay away. I couldn't stand to see my mother or father, and the house was barely fit to live in. It wasn't just its appearance, it was the smell—thick, stale marijuana smoke had been absorbed into the furniture. I would go to the park late at night. I stayed out until five in the morning, anywhere, so I didn't have to go home. Sometimes I fell asleep wherever I was, or I'd just walk around and around. No one seemed to miss me.

I never ever had time to study. I missed a lot of classes, many of them while talking to my guidance counselor. The counselor called

my father, who told him I was exaggerating. There was a time when I just gave up hope. I didn't know what to do. There was not a single good outlook: my mother is a mess; we live in a dump. My life is never going to change; when I turn eighteen I'm going to be a bum.

I flushed her marijuana down the toilet many times. Once she caught me and beat me pretty badly. I told her that I was trying to save her. She lost it completely, and dragged me to the police station. She told an officer that I had come home with marijuana, that I was an addict and she couldn't do a thing with me.

When I was allowed to speak to the officer alone, I told him to put me in a foster home, because my mother didn't want me. My concern was being happy, and if I had to leave home I would. The next morning I was packed and ready to go. When I walked into the kitchen with my suitcase my mother was on the telephone, laughing loudly and telling my girlfriend, Cecily, about the prank she had pulled last night. Mom thought the police incident was the funniest thing.

Cecily said, "Your mother needs help. She's not normal." When my mother started to hallucinate and imagine that neighbors were following her, I had to agree. I told Cecily that I was scared. I also told my aunt, who took my mother to the hospital.

At first they put her in the mental ward. After a week the doctors established that she was not insane but was suffering from drug-related behavior. The minute the decision was made to move my mother from the hospital to a rehabilitation program, Dad disappeared. He was afraid, because he had been her chief supplier.

I was left to call clinics and answer their questions: When had she started using drugs? Which drugs? Had she ever been treated for drug abuse? Where? What drugs was she using now? I prepared a long list: marijuana, methadone, heroin, a lot of prescription drugs I didn't recognize—bags of them in small bottles.

Many of the places did not take me seriously, because I was only fourteen years old. One administrator thought the whole thing was a joke. This time Cecily's parents helped get my mother admitted, but I was responsible for getting clothes to the rehab center and for visiting her.

The entire three months my mother was in the rehabilitation center my father left me alone. I took care of the house and decided which bills needed to be paid immediately and which ones could wait. Not only was the house falling apart, it was dirty. I cleaned it top to bottom. Some friends came over and we painted my room, the living room, and the kitchen. I made lists of hundreds of things that had to be fixed.

I figured if I had so many adult responsibilities, I could drive the car, too. I got tired of waiting for cabs. Once I realized I could drive, I never considered taking a cab again. I used the car to take the dog to the vet, to pick up food, and to visit my mother. Fortunately, I didn't get caught—or worse, have an accident and harm someone.

While my mother was in the rehab clinic, I neglected everything I had enjoyed doing. I gave up my spot on the varsity soccer team and stopped working on the school newspaper. My life was my mom, and that was what I lived each day for. I made lists of things I had to do for my mother when I returned from visiting her.

I finally collapsed in school, from a combination of doing too much and not sleeping. I was hospitalized for a week, because there was no one to take care of me at home. After I got out I still didn't sleep, because I was afraid of what was going to happen next.

I know my mother's mad at me, because I told her she would only be in the hospital for two months, but the doctor told me that she needed more time. She begged me and cried, "Only you can take me out." But I didn't. I was afraid I couldn't handle any more responsibility.

I guess I thought Mom would be perfect when she came home. I thought she would be happy about how well I had taken care of things and about how great the house looked. I was wrong. Coming out of rehab, my mother doesn't really know what's going on. I try not to take advantage, because I don't want to push her down again.

I want to be there for her, because Dad isn't. I could be there more, but it's really hard to look at her the way she is and remember the way she was when I was young. I often wish she hadn't gone. At least she was a person before rehabilitation. Now she's a zombie. Before, she would go out. She may have been loud and obnoxious and rude, but she did do things. She talked to me. We would fight over little things, like most families do. But she doesn't care anymore. The doctor warned me she would be different for a while, but this nothingness is hard to take.

I went to Alanon, because a friend of mine has an alcoholic mother and he attends weekly meetings. At first I thought I didn't need support, that my situation was totally unique. It isn't. I know this sounds terrible, but it's comforting to know that other people struggle, too. They have good advice, and I'm following it.

I'm playing soccer and writing for the school newspaper again. I keep an eye on my mother like I always did, but now what I have to do comes first. My grades are improving, and I don't miss classes anymore.

Dad visits. He comes back and stays a few days, until it gets too intense, and then he leaves. He still supports us; he's not mean enough to abandon us completely. He says he's moving back, but I don't really think he will. He doesn't speak to me. He has a right to be mad at me for using the car when I don't have a driver's license, but I'm mad at him for leaving me to make all the decisions about my mother. I haven't had the guts to tell him how I feel about that, but I will.

FACTS TO FOCUS ON

- Having a parent who is addicted to alcohol or other drugs is not unusual. In the state of New Jersey alone, it is estimated that close to a million people use illegal drugs. However, drug use by a parent affects every member of the family. Husbands, wives, and children are often abused or neglected by the parent who takes drugs.

- Judd Lawrence had too many responsibilities that rightfully belong to adults, not teenagers. In taking charge of the house and assuming the full burden of having his mother admitted to a clinic he was attempting to handle problems that were beyond his experience and abilities. It's no wonder he collapsed under the strain.

- A person needs a clear head and a well-rested body to withstand the extra demands of a drug-abusing parent. Good nutrition also guards against illness in anxiety-ridden situations like Judd's.

- Teens with drug-abusing parents sometimes feel they are the cause of the problem. For the longest time, Georgette Bleeker was convinced that she and her siblings were responsible for their father's addiction. She believed her father. "He blames his drinking on us. He says we are in the way; we put too much stress on him. We cost him too much money. He talks to us as if we're a burden to his life."

- Under the same circumstances, different children may react differently. Georgette's sister, Lillian, says that her father's drinking doesn't bother her. "I ignore him. When he gets crazy I tune him out. I pretend he's a television set that I can switch off."

- Teenagers usually don't have much control over parents who are out of line. Kim Lakeland talks about her alcoholic father: "When he is really drunk he threatens my mother. Sometimes she has to throw cold water or hot tea at him to shock him, but that just makes it worse. Then he grabs her and slams her against the closest wall. It's horrible to watch. When I was younger, I used to beat on my father's arms or legs to try to get him to stop. Now I'm smarter, and I'm afraid. I back way off and do my best to stay out of their way.''

■ When a parent uses drugs, it affects a child's life in every way. In school, problems are bound to crop up. A guidance counselor may be able to rearrange a student's schedule and explain the situation to the teachers. Have someone help lighten the burden at school until the crisis is under control.

■ When teachers become aware of a situation, most will be accommodating. They will reschedule tests and find time to tutor a student if necessary.

■ Telling a teacher or guidance counselor is the first step toward making life manageable. These people know how to locate other help you may need outside school.

If the counselor contacts a government agency for help, a family conference will be arranged. Most parents will come in with you for an evaluation, rather than be ordered by the state to appear. Drug-abusing parents who do not seek help are then threatened by the possibility of the teenager's being taken away from them and placed in another—safer—environment.

MOVING IN THE RIGHT DIRECTION

■ In addition to having constant anxiety about a parent's mood or behavior, teens whose parents use drugs feel everything from abandonment and anger to shame and embarrassment. It's okay to feel this way about a parent's behavior when it is illegal and unacceptable.

■ If one of your parents is addicted to alcohol or another drug, you should recognize that many professionals believe that the tendency toward alcoholism is inherited.

■ Teenagers should not be primary caregivers. Don't try to take charge of the family. Don't be mother and father, chief cook, and storyteller to younger siblings. And don't drop the activities you enjoy. When a young person abandons the things he enjoys, as Judd did, a sense of hopelessness can take over.

■ Some teenagers still remain hopeful even under extreme conditions. Beth Fachler believes that one day her mother will stop drinking. "If my mother ever stops drinking, I hope for little things that we never had. It would be nice to eat a breakfast or dinner together. It would be nice not to have blankets all over the living room couch as if it were a bedroom, which it often is for my mother."

■ Having a parent who abuses drugs or abuses you is good reason for feeling anxious, or even depressed. Says fifteen-year-old Richard Sweig, "I can't talk to my father, because he smokes dope. His mood swings are so outrageous. He's happy one minute, nuts the next. He says he's not doing cocaine anymore, but I'm not so sure. I avoid him."

■ It's not easy to stand up to a parent who abuses drugs. Beth Fachler knows that, too. "I always say I will talk to my Mom, but I'm afraid. Even though she has never hit me, I'm afraid she will lose control if I mention her drinking. I talk to my older sister and my aunt."

■ Teenagers can—and should—decide that a situation will not get the best of them. Like Beth and Richard, teens who cannot confront their parents must seek other help. Often, in helping yourself you will discover ways to convince a drug-addicted parent to start therapy or rehabilitation.

■ Many towns and schools have special support groups for teenagers. A group of peers can be immensely helpful during difficult times, and often long after. Don Haskins, age fourteen, is a member of Alateen, a group of teenagers who have drug-abusing parents. Alateen is a branch of Alcoholics Anonymous that meets regularly in most cities around the country.

"Right now I am the only one in my family who is in AA," says Don. "I go to Alateen at least once a week. I don't see myself as ever becoming an alcoholic, but I know it could happen to me. One of my biggest dreams is to have a happy family, and I know that doesn't happen if you drink.''

■ Remember that you are the most important person in your life. When the adults around you are not capable of looking out for your welfare, you must do it yourself.

6.

HOLLY AND ME

"Now if I date, I'm not looking so much for

myself as I am for my daughter," explains

Jackie Luis, the spunky teenage mother of

one-year-old Holly.

*B*efore I gave birth to Holly, I had not accumulated the required number of high-school credits for my junior year. I had to do home-bound study—a tutor came to the house—after the baby was born. I completed my senior year in a special high school with other teenage mothers. You study at your own speed and receive your high-school diploma as soon as you have earned enough credits.

[Jackie's eyes fill with tears as she talks about not finishing high school with her old friends.] I missed the class trip, the prom, and all the parties. I wasn't told about any of it, and that wasn't fair. I should have been invited.

My girlfriends couldn't believe that I was going to have this baby, that I was going to give up the shape I was in. I worked out regularly,

and had an almost perfect figure. I told them that if you play, you pay.

I'm not like other girls who go out, have sex, and don't accept the responsibility. It wasn't that I was so sexually active. I had only one partner before Ken. He and I dated for months before I gave in. He pestered me and made me feel like such a baby that I couldn't stand it. He wanted to, so I finally said okay. I wasn't really doing it for me; I was doing it for him. I was sixteen.

Ken didn't find out I was pregnant until six months later. I called and called his house. I left message after message for him to call me.

He never returned my calls—until I told his sister why I was calling. That got his family's attention. Ken called back. His mother called; even his father called. Nobody wanted me to keep this baby.

My family was dead set against the pregnancy from the beginning. My mother told me no guy would ever want to go out with me or marry me if I had someone else's baby. She kept trying to convince me to have an abortion. She called her friends and, if they didn't believe in abortion, hung up. If they believed in it, she talked to them for hours. They became her best friends. My mother even called my friends to get them to convince me to have an abortion. She offered to send me to "the best," as she put it, for the abortion and then to Hawaii for a couple of weeks on a vacation. She told me she would fix my car or buy me a new one. I told her money didn't justify murder to me.

I was so upset. I couldn't sleep or eat. I thought I was going crazy. To keep everyone quiet and off my back I said I would get an abortion. The night after I agreed to end the pregnancy, my family had a huge celebration dinner. There was tons of food, but I couldn't eat a bite. I left home the following day. My mother was so angry that I had lied to her that she wouldn't let me come back. My whole family disowned me. I had only me to get me through the next horrible, lonely months.

I spent one month in a welfare hotel. I barely ate. I had very little money, so I survived on Honey Nut Cheerios and tap water. When I took a shower I had to have someone with me, because I passed out from not eating properly. For the rest of my pregnancy I moved around from place to place.

Jane, my girlfriend from the welfare hotel, had to take me to the hospital several times. I had a heart murmur, low blood count, everything you can imagine. Nothing happened to Ken. He was off somewhere going about his normal business. He's twenty-one, and his parents let him live at home. He was working, earning money, and eating three meals a day while I was scrounging to keep my baby. I don't know how I delivered a healthy baby.

Jane and I went to childbirth classes together. I was her coach and she was mine. My sister was in the delivery room, too. I needed both of them.

Holly and I are managing better now, but not as well as I would like. We live in a government-run apartment and inspectors come to check its condition. The housing agency helps me with my rent, but I have to pay for the heat, electricity, and telephone. What the state gives me just pays those bills. If I want to get Holly extras like clothing or a toy, I babysit for my girlfriends to earn the money.

Ken doesn't help us. He doesn't take Holly, or give me money for her. Every little penny counts. I'm in debt to my mother and my

sister. Diapers cost money; food costs money—there is never enough. I buy diapers instead of putting gas in my car, so we don't go to a lot of places.

I'm taking Ken to court this week. He could help if he wanted to, but he doesn't. I hope the judge will order him to pay us something. We were supposed to go last month, but his lawyer cancelled.

Sometimes I sit back and realize that I didn't know what I was thinking about when I was pregnant. I did some babysitting when I was younger. It was fine. But with other people's kids, well, you leave. Your own baby is with you twenty-four hours a day, whether you like it or not. If I go anywhere with my girlfriends, it's a question of who wants to sacrifice and stay in with the babies while the rest of us go out. At the park I have to watch Holly every second, to be careful the bigger kids don't hurt her. At the beach, who is going to keep an eye on her—say, if I fell asleep in the sun?

I have to be responsible every single minute of every day. When I have had enough, there is no other parent or person to give me a break. I take Holly pretty much everywhere I go, except for an hour here or an hour there, when my sister or my mother watch her.

I feel like a bad parent if I take Holly out with me in the evening, even to a friend's house. She sleeps on the bed, then I pick her up and take her home in the car with me. But it doesn't seem right being out with the baby at midnight. I don't feel good about it.

Once this year I couldn't stand it anymore and called Ken. I didn't ask him, I *told* him that he had to take Holly for the weekend. I drove an hour to his house and handed him his daughter. I have had one weekend of freedon in a year, one weekend when I didn't have to get up at five forty-five, and be on guard constantly so nothing would happen to her.

Whatever I thought was going to happen after Holly was born didn't happen. Her father didn't marry me. I thought he would. I would rather have been married a while before having a baby. I don't like being a single mother and going home to nobody. It's very lonely. When I can afford it, I buy family packs of meat and then look at them and ask myself, "Why?" There's only Holly and me.

I wish I knew what our lives were going to be like. I was offered a good job cleaning houses, but I couldn't take it, because I can't leave Holly. If it was up to me I wouldn't be on welfare or getting rent assistance from HUD. My pride used to be way up there, but I had to drop it so I could keep my baby.

I can't move in with my mother, because she and I don't agree on anything. I know there are people out there who need the welfare money and housing more than I do, but living with my mother is not possible. She criticizes everything I do. She says I'm going to wind up like her—having kids, raising them alone, marrying the wrong guys, and getting divorced.

Sometimes I get angry and yell at Holly, but I know it's not her fault. I don't throw anything in her face. I don't say the things to her that my mother said to me. She was constantly telling me that I was a mistake and she wished she had never had me. Holly was a mistake to everyone but me. I love her.

If I'm going to carry a baby for nine months, I'm not going to give her up. She's part of me, and that part of me belongs to me. I don't believe in abortion or adoption. They may be right for other people, but I couldn't do it. People have to do what's right for them. I'm going to love this baby and give her everything I never had. I don't know how. I have to think about every little thing I buy.

I had Holly's first birthday party a few weeks ago. I wanted it to be special. I didn't sleep for days, not knowing where I was going to get money for party hats and cake. My mother's already on my back because I owe her so much money; I had used all my food stamps. That didn't stop me from borrowing some more. I'm going to be begging meals from my sister and friends for another week until my food stamps come in.

If I date, I'm not looking so much for myself as I am for my daughter. If he wants me, he'll have to love Holly too. She's my life now; she's what I'm living for. She keeps me going. I don't want some guy throwing her in my face. I have a new life with Holly. Sure, I'm jealous of my friends who come and go as they please. This is not what I would want if I had been given other choices, but I'm trying as hard as I can.

FACTS TO FOCUS ON

■ "Who's doing it with whom, and when, is the hottest topic of conversation in my school," reports Jack Latham, age sixteen. More than 25 percent of fifteen-year-old women and 50 percent of seventeen-year-old women have had intercourse. The fact that many teens, perhaps some of your closest friends, are having a sexual relationship may put pressure on you.

There are certain things you just don't do simply because your friends are doing them. Intercourse is right up there at the top of the list, along with using drugs, driving drunk, and making suicide pacts.

■ Pregnancy can occur the first time a female has intercourse, whether she is twelve or seventeen. There have been reports of pregnancies in girls as young as nine.

■ Because of federal budget cuts to schools, fewer classes are available today to educate teens about abstinence, condom use, and other safe methods for avoiding pregnancy and sexually transmitted diseases. Be sure you get very good birth control guidance *before* you become sexually active.

■ One out of three girls who are sexually active will become pregnant before the end of their teen years, according to a 1986 issue of the journal *Family Planning Perspectives*. In fact, women ages fifteen to nineteen are having more babies than ever before.

The actual numbers are scary: more than three thousand teenage girls become pregnant each day. That's well over 1 million every year.

■ Being pregnant as a teenager is an emotionally wrenching experience. In addition, it is physically risky to both the mother and the baby. Babies of teenage mothers often do not do as well as babies who have been carried by older mothers.

■ Teenage mothers who decide to keep their babies do so alone, because the father rarely sticks around to be a parent. As one teenage boy put it, "Guys who get girls pregnant are out of there. They don't want to talk to the girls again. They don't want to think about it. They want to believe that it never happened. For the most part, it's not love; they're just doing it for fun."

■ Most young girls end up like Jackie on their own or living with their parents, getting little or no financial support from the baby's father. Many go on welfare and become dependent on food stamps and other federal or state-funded nutrition programs. Too many teenage mothers spend the rest of their lives at or below the poverty level, anxious about how they will provide for their children.

■ Government housing for pregnant teens and teenage mothers who cannot live at home is scarce. Jackie was lucky to get her own apartment. The waiting period for HUD apartments in one suburban community is two and a half years. This is typical of the wait around the country.

■ Teens who have become pregnant will tell you how difficult making decisions is. A school nurse can put a teen in touch with a network of referral programs that operate through the public-health services in most communities. In many programs, a person from the program will meet you somewhere other than at home or in school, if you prefer. A nurse or counselor will help you decide how to tell your parents that you are pregnant.

- There are a few situations in which minors can get medical treatment without parental permission. Such treatment is available for drug or alcohol abuse, for sexually transmitted diseases, and for a pregnancy test or prenatal care while carrying the baby to term, but not for an abortion.

- If a teenager wants an abortion, there are clinics whose services are free. State laws vary on whether they allow abortion without parental knowledge or consent. Call your local public health department, Planned Parenthood office, or the National Abortion Federation Hotline, at (800) 772-9100, to find out your state's laws.

- Although Jackie did not choose either abortion or adoption, both options are possibilities for teenage girls faced with pregnancy. To be safe, an abortion must be performed within the first twelve weeks of pregnancy, by a licensed doctor in a clean, authorized clinic or hospital.

- Many teenagers get pregnant for emotional reasons they don't even understand. They may come from abusive or alcoholic families or from families in which their self-esteem has been so challenged that there is none left. A baby, they think, will replace something that has been missing in their lives. Teenage mothers often view their child as their own accomplishment—one they achieved without asking permission—and no one can tell them how to raise this child.

- Instead of having more freedom and control over their lives, teen mothers have less. No matter how much support they receive from the federal government and community social service programs, most teenage mothers return home for help in raising their babies. Having a baby pulls you into your family, rather than freeing you from it. On the whole, teenage mothers end up leaving home much later in life than do their friends who have waited until marriage to have their children.

- Very few teenagers—or grown women, for that matter—realize how enormous an undertaking a baby is. Most are overwhelmed by the constant care, long hours, and hard work of child care, as well as the exhaustion and expenses they face because of it.

MOVING IN THE RIGHT DIRECTION

■ You can date a guy for years—many girls do—and not sleep with him. Guys and girls both report "hating themselves," feeling "dirty," and not feeling good about themselves after having sex when they didn't want to.

■ Throughout your teen years you will experience sexual urges and spend time thinking about having a relationship with someone who has caught your fancy. You are as likely to be anxious about having intercourse as you are about not having it.

■ Make your decision about whether to be sexually active on the basis of your own feelings, not on your partner's. Girls who feel unsure how to proceed worry too much about hurting a guy's feelings. Think before you act. And, advises Jackie, "Don't act based on what the guy is saying. He's talking for the moment."

■ There are people who can be talked into anything. "Yes" people want to be liked. In order to please, they agree to do things they don't actually want to do. You can say *no* politely. Here are some useful excuses: "Have to be home in a few minutes." "I'm not feeling well." But the best reason is always the truth: "I don't want to."

By announcing that you are not ready, you take full responsibility, whether you are the male or the female partner. Being certain leaves little room for mistakes.

■ Make your decision and stand by it. It's an adult decision. Make it wisely—and make it before you find yourself in the position of "going just a little bit further." Don't be pushed or rushed. People of all ages feel helpless when they can't control what happens to them. Sex is one area in which you can have total charge, so take your time.

■ If you have an understanding parent, bring up the subject of birth control yourself. Ask for advice. If your parents are unable to talk to you about sex, talk to a health educator at school, or go to a clinic like Planned Parenthood or the Family Health Centers. Such clinics give excellent advice in addition to supplying proper birth control measures.

■ Don't just talk about using birth control. Investigate the types of protection available, choose one, and have it on hand for when *you* decide to become sexually involved.

"If you're not ready for the huge responsibility of parenting, wear a condom, or don't do it at all," says seventeen-year-old John Aloi. A condom protects against AIDS, too. If you are not worried about contracting AIDS, you're being naive.

■ Protecting yourself against AIDS, venereal disease, and pregnancy has nothing to do with love and trust. It has to do with common sense and having respect for yourself. Protect yourself. You're that important.

■ If you have the slightest suspicion that you might be pregnant, don't wait to be sure, and don't pretend that everything is okay. Get tested immediately, so that you don't close out your choices—including having proper prenatal care so that you can deliver a healthy baby, whether you keep it or put it up for adoption.

PART III

DON'T BE DEPRESSED

*W*ithout looking very far for very long, most of us can find something to be unhappy about: the way we look, a lack of friends, not being close to our parents or family, life that is less than perfect . . . or truly horrible, as Melissa Field's was.

Like Judd Lawrence, you may expect too much of yourself, have too much responsibility piled on you for too long. His situation and the stress and anxiety it created are surely cause for depression. Jackie Luis's pregnancy and her concern for her baby's welfare caused her constant anxiety.

Left unchecked, stress and anxiety often lead to depression. One way this happens is that when people can't cope or can't reduce their levels of anxiety they start avoiding situations that produce the anxiety. Their lives become so limited that they begin to have negative feelings about themselves and frequently label themselves failures. This feeling of failure then creates depression.

Most teenage depression can also be a reaction to events or circumstances that have changed or gone wrong. Jackie's determination to be a good mother saved her from depression. Depression takes hold when you *think* the situation cannot improve. As you will see in the next few chapters, Brooke Williams and Julie Loomis initially saw no way out of their difficulties. But Tuan Hong, who had every right to be depressed, battled his illness and depression with a positive outlook.

You can't always stop yourself from feeling down, but you can stop yourself from doing something drastic. Brian didn't. His friend Jimmy tells a sad story: "Brian shot himself when his girlfriend broke up with him. Life goes on; breaking up is something you have to deal with sooner or later. It's part of life. If I had had the chance, I would have reassured Brian that Melanie wasn't everything, that he would have met another girl. Even though most people in Brian's situation would think 'What a crock—no way, this was the only girl for me,' it still feels good to hear it. And it might have made the difference between Brian's being alive and being dead today."

The idea that suicide is related to loving someone, or loving someone too much, is a mistaken belief. Suicide is selfish and has absolutely nothing to do with love. Contrary to what many think, slashing your wrists, swallowing pills, or firing a gun into your head is not brave. These are the acts of a coward, a weak person who has simply copped out rather than waiting out or trying to brighten a black period in his life.

It is perfectly normal to feel angry at a person who tries to kill himself or succeeds in doing it. People who kill themselves are not heroes. Don't glorify them or praise their act. Suicide makes no sense. "My best friend tried to kill herself in eighth grade," recalls Nancy Green. "Toby slit her wrists. I think she was lonely. She realized later that what she did was pretty stupid. Toby has terrible scars—scars she will have all her life. It's hard to cover them. People always ask her what they are. You can't wear long sleeves when it's ninety degrees."

A period of depression often follows not only the suicide of someone you're close to, but also the "natural" death of someone you love. It's healthy and normal to grieve over and feel sad about such a powerful loss. Some people adjust faster than others do. If a depression caused by someone's death lingers longer than six months, find a professional who can explore the loss with you.

Sometimes depression stems from a far less dramatic loss than a suicide or the natural death of a parent, grandparent, sibling, or close friend. In one typical scenario, a family moves and the teenager in it is forced to leave her best friend, her spot on the gymnastics team, and her reputation as a fun-loving, great person. How, she wonders, will she ever survive, ever make new friends? She doesn't feel like making the effort.

Or suppose that a brother or sister has an illness or handicap that demands most or all of your parents' time and energy, so that they scarcely know you exist. Any of these situations can bring on depression.

The years between fifteen and nineteen are cited by the National Institute of Mental Health as one of the peak periods for the onset of serious depression. Having a serious depression during those years also increases the likelihood of substance abuse later on.

SIGNALS OF DEPRESSION

Some signs of stress and anxiety are the same as those of depression. The difference is that with depression the symptoms are more intense and continue for long periods, often months and months.

Are you using drugs—this includes alcohol—to escape or avoid what is bothering you?

Are you sexually active without being emotionally involved, or without paying attention to the consequences?

Are you stealing? Lying?

Are you starving yourself or binge eating? Are you overly concerned about getting fat?

Do you have physical problems that no doctor can pinpoint?

Have you lost interest in activities you used to find exciting?

Have you lost your energy and drive? Do you feel lazy? Have you slowed down?

Are you becoming a living, breathing couch potato, spending all your time in front of the television set?

Are you alone most of the time, rather than with friends or family?

Are you having trouble sleeping?

Are you fighting with friends? Losing friends?

Do you get angry easily and often? Do you have raging outbursts?

Are you failing in school when you had been doing fine?

If you find yourself saying "yes" or hesitating before saying "no," it may be wise to think about how you feel. Any one signal, or a group of them, could mean that depression is brewing. When depression causes you to act in peculiar ways, to engage in risky activities—or complete inactivity—it is time to take stock. Sometimes the reason for being depressed is clearcut; but at other times it may not be so easy to figure out.

A COMPLEX EXAMPLE

Cissy Hart's pattern of avoiding school indicates that a major depression has a firm hold on her. On the surface, this fifteen-year-old's problem appears to be twofold: she's too bright for her classes, and she has few friends. However, neither fact is the crux of the problem. Cissy says, "I don't like to go to school. I don't like to get up."

Her excuse sounds like this: "Every class is murder. I can tell you before I go to school what will happen in my classes, what notes will be taken, how far we will go, and what the homework will be. I decided that if I can do all that, why don't I just bring my books home and do it myself?

"No one could say anything, because I was getting all A's. I was doing better than most of the kids who were in class every day. I started staying home from school in sixth grade," says Cissy. "Seventh and eighth grades are nasty grades; the kids are backbiting and mean, so I went as little as possible. My feelings were getting stepped on all the time.

"Since my mother leaves the house before dawn and my father doesn't live with us, it was easy to call my mother with an excuse. For a long time she bought the argument that I was having different illnesses. In eighth grade, I missed thirty-nine excused days. What could she say? The absences weren't affecting my schoolwork."

Cissy has an eating disorder called bulimia, which is caused in great part by the absence of her parents. Her mother was away long hours at her job and when she was at home still thought about work; her father had moved out of state and remarried. Cissy filled her emotional emptiness with food. Young girls who are depressed often use bingeing and purging to wipe away loneliness. Weight problems deeply affect a person's feelings about themselves and for many, like Cissy, direct the course of their lives.

A STRONG WARNING

People usually experience depression as a loss of vitality and energy. In depression there is a void or a missing ingredient in your life. It can feel like an empty hole inside you, boredom, or an overwhelming sadness.

Keep your perspective when trying to understand what is upsetting you. If you were unhappy about a test grade or your boyfriend and lost your appetite for a day or two, that's not cause for alarm. If you skipped classes one day because it was the most gorgeous spring day you've ever seen or because you needed a day to catch up on your work, don't be concerned. But if you have been cutting out or lying to your parents and teachers on a regular basis, then you may be depressed. Likewise, if you feel blah or angry at the world for days and days, you should do something to correct the problem.

Distracting yourself will get you through short periods of depression. Take yourself to a movie, start a new project, listen to music, or read a book or magazine. Exercise is a natural way to lift your spirits, because during exercise the body produces chemicals that help us relax and feel content. Another way to stop thinking about your own problems is to help someone else.

If you are having long periods of depression, it's important to tell your parents and ask for their help. Most parents don't realize when their teenagers are suffering. As you will read in the next chapters, Brooke Williams had the right idea. She knew something was wrong and let her mother know it. Julie Loomis, on the other hand, allowed her depression to take over her life. Depression is a strong warning that some aspect of your life needs fixing. Unfortunately, the major cause of suicide in teenagers over the age of fourteen is depression that these teens did not talk about and for which they therefore did not get help.

7.

ONLY THREE TIMES

At the age of fourteen, Brooke Williams

enrolled in modeling school. *"My parents and I*

thought it seemed like an easy way to make

money so I could go to college."

*W*hen I was little I was a sick kid. I had tubes in my ears, my tonsils taken out, and every kind of cold, flu, and infection known to man. One time when I was about seven, I was nauseous for hours and hours, and my mother showed me how to throw up. It wasn't like "sick" motherly advice; I was horribly sick to my stomach. She thought if I threw up I would feel better. I didn't think about it again until last year.

At my modeling school you are weighed and measured before every session. I never thought that I needed to lose weight, but the school did. "You're too developed for runway modeling. For television commercials you need to work on your weight. That's where the money is anyway," the director told me. There wasn't much weight for me to lose, but when the head of the school says to take off five or ten pounds, you do it if you want him to get you work.

I check my weight constantly. At first I lost, but then it stopped coming off. Making myself throw up just popped back into my head.

I thought, okay, this works, but I had no idea what it would evolve into. I started throwing up off and on two or three times a week, but then I was doing it two or three times a day until I lost the rest of the ten pounds. I told my mother. I saw a therapist, but I never really got treated for my bulimia. Bulimia is a symptom of other problems that we didn't fix, obviously.

I stop for a month or so, but as soon as I gain three or four pounds I start again. I tell myself, "Don't do that." I am very good. Unfortunately, I'm a professional. I can walk outside, throw up in a flower bed, and come back inside and no one will know. You get so good you can throw up anywhere you choose. If you know what you're doing you won't look any different, won't make any noise. I don't make a sound.

Since I told my mother, everyone sort of knows, but it's like alcoholism—no one says anything. It's very weird. I never had to stop, because no one confronted me with it. My mother didn't pressure me; she stayed calm.

I had lost what was a lot of weight for me and was getting really thin. I thought I would put it aside, but I felt powerful. I was in control. Eating was the only thing over which I had any power. You get spurred on by the control. It's very addictive. You become obsessed: Am I going to eat today? How do I look? What am I going to wear? Your focus becomes anything and everything that has to do with how you look. As the scale goes down, your clothing fits and looks better.

Your life becomes centered around bingeing and purging, until finally you don't think about anything else. I sometimes believe that if I go swimming, water will get in my pores and I'll gain weight. I would never eat a sub sandwich, because I imagine the sandwich, long and fat, traveling down my arm and blowing up the skin like a balloon. When you start throwing up, you have no idea where it will lead.

You start off slow, thinking you're just going to try it. But it gets to the point at which you really can't quit. I try and try in every way that I can. I tell myself I will eat and not throw up. As you eat you think "I'm not hungry anymore," and then panic sets in. Oh my God, you say to yourself, I'm going to gain weight. So you throw up. It's completely consuming.

I love food—fast food, fries, and doughnuts. I have a bad sugar and chocolate habit. I hardly ever eat meals. If I do, it's noodles or spaghetti, carbohydrates, breads, candy, and chocolate. I have a sweet tooth. If you deprive yourself of those kinds of things for a long time, you get really hungry.

There is a ritual to the process. I sit on my bed, cross my legs, turn on the TV, and stare at it. Food is everywhere. You're eating and eating and eating. You get up, go in the bathroom, and puke your guts out. You can't get all the food out in one throw up. You have to throw up many times, to be sure that you get up every little piece. Some foods don't throw up. I nearly killed myself once trying to get some chunky cereal out of my system. It all balled up and stayed down.

Recently I began bingeing and purging heavily again. When you're in this pattern it's terrible. You think you are the only one on earth who does it. I always thought there was something wrong with me, that I was different from everybody else. Eating and throwing up is really disgusting, which is what makes it more of a closet thing.

This time I didn't tell anyone. My mother thought I was over it. Mothers don't know everything. My poor mom is always burdened with my problems. I'm either terribly depressed or having trouble in school or throwing up to stay thin. I hated to tell her. And my father insists that my brother and I do everything exactly right. He was not

going to understand. Especially the second time around. I knew they were going to flip out, not because they don't love me but because that's what most parents would do.

The strange thing is that since I know so much about bulimia and I'm pretty smart, you would think I could cure myself—just stop. I'm a perfectionist, I know that, and I know that I'm part of the group that bulimia hits: above-average intelligence, white females from the suburban upper-middle class, bound for success. I'm in the group; now I have to get out.

People think that Brooke got a bad test grade and then she went to it. It's not like that. It's not that I get upset and have to eat. I get hungry. Throwing up is like a drug, it really is. You don't think about it. You don't say, "Oh, I'm so stressed today" and then eat. It's an urge, something that comes over you. You lose control, lose all sense of reason.

When a person without this problem is hungry, she just eats, and that's the end of it. But for me it's different. If a food commercial comes on television, I have to change the channel. If I see something good, I can't stop thinking about food. I have to eat, but I know that if I do eat I'm going to gain weight.

The main problem is that people don't understand. I have friends who have only thrown up once in their lives. I don't understand people like *them*. My parents say, "You have to stop right now." That's the same as telling a cocaine addict to stop. You don't. Bingeing and purging gives me a high. It feels good, because I get to eat but I don't gain an ounce.

The acids left in my body after I throw up make my skin bad. I had perfect ivory skin before last year. Lately I've been throwing up five or six times a day. My throat burns all the time. I'm getting violent headaches and dizzy spells. I'm also blacking out. That's pretty scary.

I told my mother I wanted to see my therapist again, but didn't tell her why. The therapist helped me explain to my parents. We told them together. That made confessing a little easier. Now both parents watch me. They even have my brother acting like a spy. I'm not allowed to eat sweets anymore, because once they get in my body I crave more. One doughnut can set me up to fall.

I'm not going to lie to my family. My brother asked me if I got sick after dinner the other night. I admitted it. Every time I go into the bathroom, my father stands outside the door listening. If I stay inside longer than he thinks necessary, he starts screaming, "Brooke, come out of there now. What are you doing?" I usually tell him. At least I'm not lying. That would screw up my ever getting help.

Last year, therapy cured the symptoms temporarily, but not the problem. I hope I don't have to be hospitalized. The last couple of days, though, I've been very good . . . only three times.

FACTS TO FOCUS ON

■ In her pursuit of a modeling career, Brooke began dieting. Not being able to take off enough weight led her to believe that she was actually too fat. According to doctors, nurses, and mental-health professionals, many serious eating problems begin because of low self-esteem. The idea that you have to look pretty or that you're nothing and your peers won't like you is one of the causes that can trigger an eating problem.

■ Not feeling good about yourself is one symptom of depression. Some who feel this way think that starvation (anorexia) or bingeing and throwing up (bulimia) to lose weight will remedy real or perceived problems.

■ The patterns created by eating disorders are extremely difficult to break, as Brooke points out. Michele Durand, another teenage bulimic, explains how depressed and desperate her addiction to bingeing and purging made her: "There was never a day for over a year and a half that I did not throw up. I tried and tried to quit. I considered killing myself. I'm Catholic, but I didn't care if I went to hell. That's how bad it gets."

■ Our society is unreasonably afraid of gaining a few pounds. There is incredible social pressure to have the "perfect" body. This tremendous focus on thinness affects many young girls even before they become teenagers. A recent study of fourth-graders in San Francisco showed that their most important worry was dieting. By age nine they were already dissatisfied with their bodies. So it's no surprise that, at any given moment, about one-half of American women of all ages are dieting.

■ There is more to being overweight than eating extra helpings of mashed potatoes and ice-cream sundaes smothered in whipped cream (sounds good, huh?). Heredity plays an important role in whether you will be thin or will have a tendency to put on weight.

  If you have one overweight parent, there is a 40 percent chance that you will follow suit. If both your parents are overweight the chance doubles, to 80 percent. In other words, you could be heavy because someone in your family—a grandparent or a great-grandparent—passed on the tendency to you. The best way to keep a tendency toward gaining weight in check is to eat sensibly.

■ Movies, television, rock videos, and magazines want to make us believe that there is no such thing as being too thin. This is a dangerous philosophy, however, because females grow until about the age of sixteen and males until about the age of eighteen. It is vital to eat balanced meals that are moderate in fat content during your developing years.

■ There are emotional reasons why people eat too much and too often. Food is a form of love; it's comforting, like a close friend. If your parents are fighting, you can bury yourself in a bag of cookies or chips.

Food may also seem like a good way to get even with a parent, or to avoid making difficult decisions. If you allow yourself to get so heavy or so thin that no one will ask you out, you won't have to face any of the issues of dating or making choices about sex. In other words, an eating disorder is often used as a way of gaining control of life in an area that is troubling.

- One teen, who put on thirty pounds after her boyfriend dumped her, didn't understand the dangers of extreme dieting. "People made fun of me; they called me fatso and blimp. I wanted instant loss. I starved myself—no breakfast, two cookies for lunch, and just enough of what my mother cooked for dinner to stop the starvation feeling. I would not eat anything after six o'clock. So if I didn't eat dinner, I had to go without food until lunch the next day. I exercised vigorously every night. I lost the thirty pounds in three months. By fourteen I was a full-fledged anorexic."

- Most often, anorexia starts between the ages of twelve and eighteen. This disease is less common among boys. Anorexics can die and have died of malnutrition. If an anorexic loses too much weight and still refuses to eat, she will be hospitalized. A tube will be stuck through her nose and down her throat to feed her until she has gained a satisfactory amount of weight.

- The bulimic and the anorexic suffer from the delusion that if they can get their weight down, everything else will be all right: My parents will love me, my ex-boyfriend will rediscover me, I'll wear size-two clothing, I'll be prettier and I'll have a hundred friends.

- Bulimia, also called bingeing and purging, is closely related to anorexia. A person can be both. A bulimic eats huge amounts of food in short periods of time, often within an hour or two. After gorging, the bulimic makes herself vomit, to get rid of the calories she has consumed.

- Some bulimics, like anorexics, resort to enemas, laxatives, and diet pills. Diuretics (known as water pills) also reduce the amount of potassium in the body. Diet pills are a drug. Some, referred to as amphetamines or uppers, are often sold on the black market. These are pills you do not ever want to take.

- Many bulimics drink alcohol. Being intoxicated makes it easier for them to throw up and avoid recognizing what they are doing. So there is a risk of adding alcohol addiction to an eating disorder problem.

- Both types of eating disorders have unpleasant side effects. The most common ones include the yellowing of teeth and rapid tooth decay from the stomach acids that vomiting brings up. Also common are dry skin, hair loss, interruption of the menstrual cycle, sore throats, facial blemishes, headaches, dizzy spells, and periods of blacking out.

- A bulimic takes a chance on rupturing her esophagus every time she purges. A ruptured esophagus bleeds into the body. Holes blown in the esophagus can bleed even without the person knowing it. As a result, bulimics often throw up blood from the havoc created by their stomach acids and the wear and tear on the esophagus.

- Another major life-threatening reason for not bingeing and purging is the risk of damage to your heart. In conjunction with other elements in the body, potassium keeps the heart in its normal rhythm. If the potassium level drops too low, one chamber of the heart will beat too swiftly. Under the stress of having too little potassium, the heart can stop.

- Starving yourself or throwing up is not something to fool around with, not something to experiment with. Sara Jane Samuels, age nineteen, a recovered bulimic, explains why. "I don't know anyone who started bingeing and purging who has been able to play with it and get out. I don't know anyone who has started and not become addicted."

- Once an eating disorder takes hold, it's a long, hard pull to get away from it, usually involving years of intensive therapy. The longer an eating order persists, the more difficult it is to cure.

- Without help, the quest for thinness never seems to end. Some anorexics and bulimics are put into live-in treatment programs, often in hospitals. In such programs privileges are based on the participant's behavior. They start out under strict control. All meals are observed with everyone on a calorie count. Anorexics and bulimics alike are observed in the bathroom, until they have progressed far enough to be trusted.

■ Michele Durand describes her anorexic roommate: "She was five feet five and weighed sixty-two pounds. You saw bones in her you didn't know people had. I was afraid of her. She would not touch anything without a tissue in her hands. Every movement she made had to be exercise. If she put something in the garbage, she did deep knee bends. She chewed each bite of food twenty-three times before swallowing. She was a real trip. She had no rear end, no cheeks, no line. She could not sit on hard chairs, because her bones would break through her skin."

MOVING IN THE RIGHT DIRECTION

■ By this stage of your life you are responsible for yourself in matters of eating and personal appearance. Your parents can neither force you to eat nutritionally nor prevent you from pigging out on greasy fast foods all week.

■ Constant dieting and extreme weight loss are physically and emotionally damaging. However, there are safe, sensible ways to take off extra pounds. Proper foods and exercise can go a long way toward reducing your weight without destroying your health.

■ Those who exercise on a regular basis will have fewer weight problems. Consistent walking, fifteen to twenty minutes every day, will help keep your weight in control. In short, don't ride when you can walk.

■ There is an enormous difference between actually being overweight and simply thinking you are overweight. Look at a standardized height–weight chart, and believe what it or your doctor tells you.

■ If you truly need to lose weight and keep it off, you must change your eating patterns. Stop snacking between meals and avoid chocolate, cookies, and ice cream. Cut down on sweets and fats. Eat an apple, for instance, instead of a doughnut.

■ Losing a large amount of weight in a short period of time is not good for your body. Don't follow fad diets you read about in books or magazines. The pounds lost by crash dieting are usually regained.

■ Don't skip meals. When you do, your rate of metabolism slows and you burn fewer calories. A nutritionist or doctor should plan a diet geared to your age and stage of development.

■ If you have parents who are diet freaks, you may not be getting the nutrition your body needs.

■ If you are tempted to take diet pills, don't. They are dangerous. See a doctor instead.

■ If you think you can change the way you feel about yourself simply by losing weight, your thinking is all wrong. Be concerned if you find yourself doing any of these:

Staying on a strict diet all the time
Counting calories over and over
Weighing your food portions
Avoiding places that serve food
Being afraid to be around food
Loosing weight but feeling that what you have lost is never enough

■ Be sure you are not using food as a weapon or as a means of coping with tough problems. Be watchful if you are using food as a source of comfort; that is, do you eat more when you are nervous, unhappy, or angry?

■ Anyone who is eating compulsively, bingeing and purging, starving—or just thinking about it—should be asking, "what is bothering me?" Eating disorders block out emotions, because their focus on food is so complete. "You're too busy being obsessed with what you eat to have time for feelings. That's probably why it's so hard to quit," notes Sara Jane Samuels.

■ It's very difficult to spot a bulimic, because bulimics often carry their normal weight. You can go for years wanting help, but not get a response unless you ask. Have a parent take you to a psychiatrist or psychologist or to a clinic that treats eating disorders.

■ The telephone book lists crisis hot lines and eating-disorder hot lines or groups. Check under "Counseling" or "Mental Health" for an eating disorder specialist or center near you. Call a local hospital and ask if it has a program. Most of these programs do not require parental consent for teenagers to participate.

■ No one is perfect. It is far more important to be healthy than to be thin. If safe attempts to lose weight don't work the first time, keep trying. As soon as you begin to do the best you can with what you have, you'll find new things to do, and food and being fat or food and thinness will be something you won't worry about all the time.

8.

TO JULIE; LOVE, DAD

"When I heard that my best friend's older sister had smoked pot with my father, I thought it was the greatest thing in the world. What did I know? I was barely a teenager. It was the same year my parents had divorced," explains Julie Loomis.

*S*hortly after my parents split up, I found rolling papers and marijuana in a kitchen drawer. I was thrilled to death. I had just celebrated my thirteenth birthday.

It didn't take a private investigator to discover that there was always pot in my house. I made good use of the unending supply. I smoked twice a day—after school and again in the evening. It wasn't long before my friends began stopping at my house for a joint before school. Being high made classes bearable. I smoked pot daily for years.

By the time I was fifteen, my father was getting high with us. He said it was better to smoke at home than to get caught outside. One Christmas a bag of marijuana gaily wrapped in Santa Claus paper was stuffed into the foot of my stocking. The gift tag read, "To Julie; Love, Dad." My father was correct in thinking I would love that present. I bragged about it to my friends each time I rolled a joint and shared it with them.

I lived with my father and his young girlfriend, who was half his age. She wanted to be my friend, not my mother. They knew I missed my mother, but that didn't change their schedule. They were hardly ever home. When they were, they hid in the bedroom to use harder drugs, as if I didn't know.

I had parties most afternoons, many of which lasted until well into the night. Like my friends' parents, my father traveled, or didn't bother to come home. Not that he would have cared if he had walked in on a party. I'm positive he would have joined us.

My mother had no idea what was happening. If she had known, she would have had a fit and insisted that I come live with her, I'm sure of that. Somehow I ended up living with my father after the divorce. I still haven't figured out why. I don't remember—probably I don't want to—much of what went on during the divorce. I just remember that it was horrible.

Once I started smoking pot, I stopped studying. I stopped caring about learning. In eighth grade I began using cocaine, too. Cocaine was pretty much a habit all the way through. At first I didn't need much, but by tenth grade my habit was getting expensive. To avoid the expense I picked my friends carefully from those who had large quantities of the drugs I wanted.

I had to repeat tenth grade, and when I couldn't get through it the second time around my father enrolled me in the local private school. I didn't want to go and started to party more than before, if that's possible.

I was at a standstill, but no one seemed too concerned—certainly not me. I thought I was having a great time. If my father noticed, he

was smart enough to understand that he couldn't do anything about my drug use. After all, he had been my first supplier. My friends' parents weren't around much either; they had high-pressure jobs with long hours. And those who were home didn't want to know; they pretended nothing was happening. Even if we had gotten caught, I don't think it would have stopped us.

Of all my friends, I had the least to worry about. My father was concerned only with his own good time. I stayed away from my mother. She asked me to visit, to spend the night or stay for the weekend, but I made up excuse after excuse so I wouldn't have to see her. I know I hurt her each time I refused. I saw her only when I had to: for Mother's Day, Christmas, and Thanksgiving. I could pull myself together to get through a few hours without arousing her suspicions. I felt bad, because I know my mother loved me and cared about me more than my dad did. Yet I couldn't motivate myself to see her more than I absolutely had to. I could not face changing my life, and my mother would have made me do that. I was too caught up in cocaine and marijuana. I was a total addict, too afraid to think about stopping.

Nothing mattered. I didn't care about anything. I was going through life not caring. Every single day from junior high school all the way through high school and for a year after that I was high on something. I graduated from high school only because the tuition was so expensive. The school probably felt it had to give a diploma to anyone who could afford to fork over the money.

I lasted in a community college less than six months, because I continued using drugs at a steadily increasing pace. I didn't set foot in a classroom—not once. I was in bars every night until four in the morning and snorted cocaine during the day to stay awake. I left school, returned to live with my father, and found a boring clerical job. I hooked up again with some of my old friends who had progressed, like myself, to heavier use and harder drugs.

The guy I dated after my brief college career had a bad cocaine habit and my costs, like his, skyrocketed. I worked my way up to a six-hundred-dollar-a-week habit. Then I met another guy, who had a heroin habit. One morning when I had a hangover from drinking and was depressed from the night before he said he had just the thing to make me feel better. I tried heroin and fell instantly in love with it. We started making daily runs, driving an hour and a half each way to pick up heroin and crack.

My salary from my secretarial job didn't begin to cover my drug debts. I borrowed a lot of money from friends, aunts, uncles, my dad, his girlfriend, and my mother. In a way, my mother was the easiest to con. She didn't have a clue that I was an addict. I made up wild stories for her about why I needed money: an exotic vacation I had to take with my friends, an expensive dress I had to have for an office party, another major repair for my car. There were lots of phony car repairs. She was always so glad to see me that she gave it to me with no questions asked.

I never took to the streets, and I never used needles, but the damage was already done as far as my being physically addicted. I was a mess, but I fooled most people until I stopped going to work

and washing my hair. I knew I was in real trouble when I lost my car to pay my drug debts. Finally I couldn't take it anymore. When you're thirteen and starting out, you don't think it's possible to ever become an addict. Using drugs just looks like fun. It's not.

I decided I needed help. Serious help, the kind you get only in long-term rehabilitation. I had an interview and went to live in a depressing, falling-down rehab center. One year, locked in. I didn't get out very often. If someone in residence broke a rule, and someone always did, the entire group lost its passes. When you do get out for a few hours you are frisked, your urine is tested, and you are verbally grilled on your return: What did you go? Who did you see? How long did you stay? Where did you eat? To get myself straight, I lived a year in hell and hated every minute.

I want to go back to school. I'm not stupid, but there are a lot of things I don't know: basic history, math. I blew it. I can go back to school, but it's harder knowing how much time I wasted.

I think all the years I was doing drugs I never really wanted to. Drugs were just there in the kitchen drawer, in the liquor cabinet, so easy to get. I could do whatever I wanted whenever I wanted. I had so much freedom, too much for a kid. I know my father didn't care what I did, as long as I stayed in school and didn't get caught by the police. He knew I wouldn't turn him in if he kept me supplied.

My children are never ever getting involved with any of this. The surroundings in my case had a lot to do with it. I had no structure, no role model. I'm furious and angry at my dad. I'll never forgive him. I don't speak to him anymore. My father is really a jerk, but I didn't realize it at the time. I was swept up by his liberalism, when what I needed was my mother's supervision and a strong position against drugs. If I had had someone to show me the right things to do, my life would have been a whole different story.

I'm paying now, as far as friendships and relationships go. I was high for years and years every single day. You don't know what you're doing or what you want. You don't grow up while you're on drugs—and that includes heavy drinking. I was lucky: I never got arrested on the daily crack runs or picked up for drunk driving. But the results are still disastrous personally. I can't form long-lasting relationships with men or women. I feel as if I can't love anyone. My mind didn't grow the right way; I didn't mature like other people.

I've been out of drug rehab—I usually call it prison—for over a year. I don't have any urges to use drugs or drink. I'm into exercise and eating healthy foods. I realized too late that drugs are a huge waste of time and far more dangerous than I ever admitted to myself.

I know people who go into seizures from drugs and then start freebasing again an hour later. That tells you how little control a drug user has. I've had friends who died and one who is paralyzed for life from a terrible car accident that resulted from doing drugs and driving. When I think about those people I don't feel so sorry for myself.

I know what I want to do; it's just going to take me a lot longer than most people to reach my goals. And that makes me sad. I was kidding myself, thinking that I was cool and having fun. I can never get back all the years of my life I lost.

FACTS TO FOCUS ON

■ Many drugs are depressants. If you are depressed by a situation like Julie's parents' divorce, alcohol and other drugs will only depress you further. Drug use depresses you two ways. Physiologically, your body gets worn out. And if drug use gets out of control, you lead your life to get the drug, and the rest of your life falls away. You're left with a narrow life, with not much in it to give you the self-esteem you need. Drug use and alcohol consumption make depression worse, not better.

■ Some teens drink, smoke marijuana, or use crack because they feel they have to in order to fit in. The fact is that most drug users—and alcohol is a drug—don't really care about someone else's choice.

■ For every person who, like Julie when she started, thinks drug use is cool, there is one who doesn't. Says Kay Brooker, "I decided when I was thirteen that I did not want to drink. I've been drunk. I especially didn't like the next morning. I was sick."

■ Younger teens have a harder time refusing drugs. "When I was a freshman and at a party with juniors and seniors, I worried about what I wore, how I looked, what I said. I didn't know what to do about drinking," recalls Jennifer Grubb, age sixteen.

■ Your parents are your first role models. If you have a parent like Julie's dad who abuses drugs, do not follow his or her lead. Parents who smoke, overeat, or take too many prescription drugs are displaying addictive behaviors that teenagers want to avoid.

■ Children from families whose parents drink only socially and then in moderation have the fewest problems with alcohol and other drugs.

■ Drugs are often available for the asking, but they don't make you feel better. Instant highs quickly—sometimes within minutes—become depressing lows.

■ To add to your apprehension about using drugs, reconsider what you may already know. In addition to damaging the heart and brain, cocaine can cause heart attacks and sudden death. This risk remains even weeks after a person stops using the drug.

■ No one knows who will get addicted to any particular drug. People react in different ways to different amounts of substances. There are many recorded cases of deaths from a single use of cocaine or so-called designer drugs.

A person is most likely to develop a dependence on alcohol between the ages of fifteen and nineteen. Some people become "hooked" after just one drink or one toke on a joint. Today most young addicts are polyaddicted. In other words, they are addicted to more than one substance. For Julie it was first marijuana and alcohol, followed by marijuana and cocaine, then by marijuana, cocaine, and heroin.

■ Many teens, like Julie, become so involved with drugs that they don't care about school, friendships, their futures, or their lives. Depression is harder to treat when a teenager is abusing drugs.

■ Getting high every weekend to avoid the pressures of school or home is risky business. This habit is as dangerous as daily drinking. Kay Brooker feels that such behavior is "insulting to your own intelligence."

MOVING IN THE RIGHT DIRECTION

■ Be aware of what is influencing you. The views on alcohol of Edison, New Jersey, eighth grader Sylvia Ventura were printed in *The New York Times*: "Every year thousands of kids die, yet thousands laugh at the idea that it [alcohol] can be deadly. . . . One of the reasons a lot of kids get into drinking is because they grow up getting mixed messages from their parents. One minute a parent might be telling their child how bad alcohol is for them, and the next minute they'll have a beer or glass of wine in their hand." Analyze your parents' opinions, actions, and drinking habits closely, to see if they may be swaying you.

- People who resist the social pressure to use drugs get positive results. Lannie Johnson, age seventeen, explains that "there is so much pressure, but I don't care. I'm proud that I'm not involved, and I'm not embarrassed to say so. I gain a lot of respect and admiration because I have taken a stand and I stick to it. People who are embarrassed, who fudge the issue by saying, 'Well, I really don't want to,' are ashamed of their decision."

- Ask yourself why you should even bother with drugs in the first place. A lot of people drink to excuse their behavior. If you're drunk, you are not responsible for, or do not have to feel responsible for, what you do, or so the thinking goes. Others use drugs to forget the pressures they are under. "Many of my friends have academic pressure from their parents. They say, 'I can't wait until Friday to get out and drink and forget schoolwork,' " remarks Tim Clark.

- If you refrain from judging those who are using drugs and simply say "No, not for me," you probably won't be banished from the group. More likely, after a while you'll leave on your own. You'll become involved with new friends who feel the same way you do about alcohol and other drugs.

- If you start using drugs—a definite case of moving in the dead-wrong direction—you will need to cover your tracks. For example, if you're at a party with alcohol and tell your parents you were somewhere else, you will eventually need to cover up your coverup. Lies become an enormous burden, not to mention the difficulty of keeping your stories straight. It's much easier to be truthful.

- When parents feel secure that their children are not going to make problems for themselves, they are much more likely to be lenient and offer increased freedom.

- When you are in a tight spot, here are some responses that will make refusing alcohol and other drugs easier. This is one instance in which what you say doesn't have to be true; it only has to work. After you say "No, thanks," add, if necessary:

I get sick easily.
I'm not feeling well.
I have to be up early in the morning.
I have to play ball (or another sport) tomorrow.

Parent-related responses work well, too:

I have to be home early.
My parents always know.
If my parents find out, I won't be allowed out next weekend.
If my parents catch me drunk I'll be grounded for life.

9.

BEATING THE ODDS

"I think I can't handle it anymore, then I wake

up the next day and go on. I'm still here, and

the will to stay here is great,"

says sixteen-year-old Tuan Hong.

*A*t first I didn't pay much attention to the black-and-blue marks, one one day, then another. I kept on playing tennis—I'm on the high school team—and going to school. Then bruises appeared on my arms, my neck, my thighs, my back. Finally I couldn't ignore them. I had so many, for no reason—I hadn't been in any fights or walked into any doorknobs, and I don't play football.

It took several doctors and many tests before I was diagnosed correctly. When the doctor told us what was wrong with me, my mother went berserk. It was her birthday. The news wasn't a very good present. She is having a hard time dealing with my illness. She's not as strong as I am, but she's getting better. I'm a strong person most of the time.

I have severe aplastic anemia. It's like leukemia, but worse. With leukemia the body makes blood, but an antibody destroys the blood. I

don't make blood like everyone else. I will need a week of chemotherapy to kill the marrow that is in my bones so that it can be replaced with healthy marrow. I'll have a bone marrow transplant, but finding a match will be a long and difficult process.

The doctors have me on and off steroids to keep me going until they can locate a match. First I'm fat from the medication, then they take me off it and I'm thin and pale. I'm not normally fat or hairy. At one point I gained twenty pounds and grew hair like a gorilla. My best friend, Dan, can't look at me when my face blows up from the steriods. People didn't recognize me. They passed me and didn't know me. I had trouble with that, but I couldn't do anything. My friends don't want to be seen with me. When I'm with them, I feel as if they're embarrassed. I know what they're thinking; I just wish they would say it to me instead of talking behind my back.

I hear comments in the halls or around the lockers that I really don't want to hear, things like "Tuan grosses me out" or "Can you believe how bad he looks? He used to be cute." Stuff like that. Some kids just gawk at me. In class I can feel their eyes burning into the back of my head. Kids are mean. Even my so-called good friends are worried about their own images, as if being seen with me will ruin their reputations.

I told my friends to be straight with me, to be honest, but most of them can't do that. I hate the way I look when the medication is working. But I hate even more the way I'm treated. When the word got out that I was sick, some of the guys moved to another lunch table. It didn't bother me at all when I was forced to leave school. I was glad to be out of there.

When they figured out what I had, I spent two months in the hospital undergoing different kinds of experimental treatments. The doctors were trying to cure me without a transplant. These treatments didn't work. I still can't manufacture my own blood platelets. I need a lot of blood right now.

I go to the hospital every other day to have my blood tested. I practically live at one hospital or another. I'm either having a blood test or a transfusion. Most of the time, my mother goes with me. I couldn't take anyone else, because it's so boring and it takes forever. Whenever I need blood, I have to be admitted—the same forms, the same stupid papers to fill out every time. The transfusion lasts five hours, plus an hour to drive there and an hour to drive home. Lately, I have needed blood twice a week. The doctor told me I may need it more often soon. With the testing on the other days, I don't have much time for anything else. If I develop an infection, I'm hospitalized for a week or two.

I have so many limitations. I have to take precautions so that I don't get cut or badly bruised. It used to be you name it, I did it— tennis, swimming, working out, track, soccer. I was constantly on the move. A few months ago, I had what I thought was a spurt of energy and put on my jogging shorts. I wasn't halfway down the block when I thought I was going to pass out. Now I tell myself I have this disease and I have to deal with it any way I can.

I miss my friends. No one comes over; no one calls very often. My friends just left me hanging. I don't like the way they use the excuse that I'm sick and they don't want to bother me. If I want to know what's happening, I have to call one of the guys ten times just to find him home. When I do reach someone, there's silence on the line when he hears who's calling. Guilt, I suppose. I'm the same person, but they don't see that.

Dan calls once in a while, but he's too busy with tennis and soccer practice and working out to visit. I know that he's pressed for time, but he could find an hour somewhere to stop by. I miss not going around with Dan. I would be happy just to sit over at his house and be together. I tried to talk to him, but he doesn't understand. Dan thinks I'm feeling sorry for myself. It's not that at all. I simply can't keep up anymore. I don't feel sick; I just feel tired all the time. It's pretty rough.

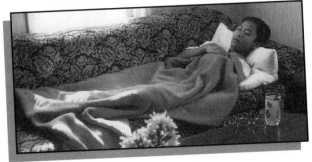

Every once in a while I try doing something with my friends, but I can only do that sometimes. It depends on whether or not I need blood. When I need a transfusion I have no energy; I spend the day on the couch. If I feel okay, I'm wrapped up in finding blood donors and starting fundraisers. I will need money to fly from Chicago to Seattle for the marrow transplant. I have to keep reminding myself that that's more important than anything else.

No one says it outright, but I know that if a suitable match isn't found and I don't have the transplant, I'll die. My brother, who was my best hope for a bone-marrow match, has been tested. He's not a match; he matches me on only half the criteria. We're testing my cousins next. I have two on one side and four on the other. Some of them are not very willing. I don't blame them, but I don't think anyone in my family wants it on his head if I die because we couldn't find a match. If we have to look for a donor outside the family, my chances are not very good. The people at the donor program told me that only one stranger out of twenty thousand would be a compatible match. Those are pretty terrible odds.

This has been going on for over a year. I think that my friends have begun to look at me and say to themselves, he really is sick. My friends avoid me totally. They have no idea how to deal with my illness. They don't know what to say or how to act. That's hard on me, because I feel as if they're neglecting me. Even if I wanted to go to a movie or on a bike ride, I can't make plans because of my schedule. I don't know from one day to the next if I'm going to be in the hospital. For the same reason, I can't go to school. Most days I probably wouldn't have the energy to get through a regular school day anyway.

Most of the time I feel isolated. Everyone seems to think that they can catch what I have. Even my dad avoids me. I know that my cousins are helping out only because they have to, not because they want to. It's not easy to be dependent on so many people—my mother, my cousins, the doctors, nurses, blood donors—but I have no choice. I used to be very independent, but when this happened to me I had to give up my after-school job too. I would feel better if I had been able to keep my job and have the extra spending money available if I wanted to use it.

On the outside I'm handling my disease, putting up a pretty good front, but on the inside I'm scared. Every time my spirits are up, it seems there's a medical setback or something negative happens. I get depressed because people look at me as if I'm not normal. I've even had people laugh at me when I don't look anything like I used to look. I bottle up my anger until I explode. I lose it and scream at my mother. She cries, but at least she's company, at least she understands. If I'm too low, which doesn't happen very often, she pulls herself together and "kick starts" me.

I want to get back to a normal life. I would be so happy if I could call Dan or one of the other guys and say, "I'll meet you at the courts or on the soccer field in ten minutes." I'd be happy if I could meet a friend for a hamburger and fries. I'd be happy if I woke up one morning feeling as if I could do any of those things.

I have plans for myself. When this is over I'm going to finish high school and go to college. I'm hoping to play tennis in the Olympics one year. I'll beat this blood business. I'll do it. I have to.

Postscript: Tuan is beating the odds and is back in school full-time. Without a transplant, he began manufacturing his own blood platelets. He has been taken off all medication and has not had a transfusion in five months. He says, "I'll have to start back at a slow pace. Before I begin anything, especially sports, I have to ask myself, 'Can I do it?' If I can't do it today, I know I'll be able to do it tomorrow."

FACTS TO FOCUS ON

■ Tuan Hong has what may be a terminal illness. Through the pain of his medical treatment, Tuan complains little. He has periods of depression, but instead of allowing depression to consume him he spends his "feeling good" time working toward goals that will help him get well.

■ It is foolish for anyone who is ill or disabled ever to give up hope. Today new medical treatment techniques, new medications, and new types of surgery are being discovered and used every day to cure illnesses and correct physical problems. The very next break-through could be the one that provides the cure or makes life more comfortable and more encouraging.

■ It is hard to accept the fact that a good friend is seriously ill. When a person has always been energetic and happy, you don't expect his life-style to change dramatically when an illness takes hold. It may take some time for the reality of someone else's limitations—or your own—from an illness or accident to sink in.

■ If someone you know is ill for a long time, it is important to be there for him. Act normally, as if nothing were terribly different or wrong. When the healthy person focuses on the illness or disability or behaves as if he were afraid of catching the disease (unless there is a real possibility of this), the patient will feel worse, even uncomfortable in the healthy person's presence.

■ It may feel strange to be with a person who looks different or can't do the things he once could because of his illness. As difficult as keeping up such a relationship may be for you, it is much more difficult for the person who has become incapacitated.

■ Being there, keeping the patient informed about friends and activities, and showing your friendship go a long way in boosting the morale of someone who is sick. A telephone call every day or a brief visit is a major event for someone who either is or feels cut off from his friends.

■ There are instances in which someone who is hospitalized, homebound, or confined to a wheelchair becomes bitter. Overtures of kindness from friends or family may be rejected if the person is experiencing a great sense of denial, if he refuses to accept what happened to him. When offers of assistance, phone calls, or friendship are refused, try again, and keep trying. Be persistent in offering your attention and support. That is exactly what someone in such circumstances needs the most. When they say no, they usually don't mean what they are saying. Try a different day, a different way.

Being cut off from friends—whether for strictly medical reasons or by choice—causes depression. Tuan needed to know that his friends still cared about him.

■ You can also suffer a bout of depression over circumstances that are far less isolating than Tuan's—for instance, because you have reached a goal or finished a project that you had been working on for a long time.

Let's say that you have spent months preparing for the opening of a play. The play proves a huge success and the reviews are raves. The play has its four-night or one-week run. What remains then is empty hours, the ones previously spent after school and in the evening rehearsing. It would be natural to experience a strong letdown. Take some time off, then look for a new project and set a new goal for yourself.

MOVING IN THE RIGHT DIRECTION

■ Solid parent–teen relationships are helpful in solving everyday problems, but for major difficulties like Tuan's they are essential.

■ More than anything else, young people suffering from illness would rather be healthy. Whenever possible, they want their friends to include them in activities, not shy away from them or treat them as if they had just landed from outer space.

■ Call as often as you did before the illness or accident. Invite your friend to join you if he is able. As one of Tuan's cousins said, "We went to a lake fishing one summer day. I was terrified that something would happen and we would be so far from the hospital or help. I knew Tuan could bleed to death if he cut himself, but I pretended fishing was the same old outing it had always been before we could drive and our dads went along."

■ Illness aside, it is virtually impossible to get through your teen years without having some periods of feeling down in the dumps and depressed, but don't confuse boredom with depression.

■ If you recognize a warning sign that you may be depressed, don't ignore it. One of the most difficult things in life is to face reality. Admitting that a condition exists or that a particular situation is horrible is the most important step in accepting the condition and feeling better about the situation—and yourself.

■ In some instances a person won't know how to handle disappointment. Given time, most people figure out a way. And over time, the disappointment will come to seem much less important.

■ Feelings of worthlessness are not uncommon during the teen years. Don't believe for one second that you are worthless. If the feeling persists, talk it out.

■ A situation that seems hopeless to you may not seem that way to someone else. Another person may add new insights and be able to offer workable, perhaps even better, solutions than you thought possible.

■ Nothing in life stays the same. The seasons change, friends change, and teachers change each year. One good grade can change the way you think about a class, one invitation to a party can alter the way you feel about friends, and one good book can change your attitude about reading.

■ It is essential for everyone—whether healthy or ill—to keep their hopes and dreams alive, as Tuan did. By facing the future with a positive attitude, Tuan had something to look forward to, to struggle for, to achieve.

EPILOGUE

TAKING CHARGE

*J*anet Augustine's circumstances forced her to take charge of herself as a preteen, when her parents divorced. "My mom was never baking chocolate-chip cookies when I got home from school. She came home from work hours later, sometimes long after dinner. I grew up very fast."

Having a significant amount of responsibility creates varying degrees of stress, anxiety, and depression. As the stories in this book have demonstrated, teens handle pressure differently. Some get angry and lash out. Others become quiet and withdrawn. Here's how one sixteen-year-old boy copes with his burdened life: "I plan, but I still have to go day by day, because problems come up and I can't do what I set out to do. I keep myself busy. That's how I keep sane."

Another teen, Jennifer Sheedy, says, "I laugh when things go wrong or when things are out of my control. I could get upset and stressed out, but that wastes too much energy."

Still others act recklessly, becoming involved with drugs or other unacceptable behavior to escape the real problem. Do you know how you react or would react, if you had a major personal setback or were placed in a seemingly impossible situation?

Throughout your life you have been given the idea that you shouldn't be hurt or unhappy. You've probably watched your parents get rid of their own problems or pain in one way or another. For a headache they pop a pill; after a tough day they may guzzle a drink or two. You could easily and mistakenly think that there's a quick fix for anything that bothers you. The teenagers you have read about had considerable emotional pain. Those who took short-cut remedies found that they backfired. In spite of their extreme difficulties, every one of these teens was smart enough to avoid using the ultimate escape from problems—suicide. There is nothing righteous or glamorous about suicide. It's an unacceptable solution to what is usually only a temporary problem.

When someone kills himself, an outpouring of love and adoration flows from those left behind. News coverage shows a display of warmth and caring for this person. His deeds are praised and sadness prevails for the accomplishments he will never achieve. What you do not see in all this is the rage and anger at the victim. There is plenty of it. A sense of betrayal and hurt lingers long after the mourning stops. The thought "how dare he?" prevails forever. If you are ever so miserable that you start considering whether to end your life, recognize that people will be sad, but they will also be furious. Your action will be resented. You will win attention for a short time, but the long-term effect will be negative. Suicide corrects and accomplishes nothing.

Think about the last time you were in a good mood. How long did it last? Two hours? Five minutes? What about in a bad mood? One hour? A few days? The point is that things are always shifting and changing. Whatever your predicament, there's a sensible solution to it. Think through the consequences and talk over the problems.

TAKING CHARGE MEANS FINDING HELP

It takes great strength of character to recognize that you need even a little bit of help and to seek it out. Some teenagers think that exposing their problems to others is wimpy or will be perceived as weakness. In fact, the opposite is true. There's no doubt that it's difficult to pour your heart out to someone you don't know well. But once you take the first step and approach an adult or a friend with your problem, the awkwardness of the situation fades.

We would all like to have parents in whom we can confide, who take us seriously. Only a handful of teenagers are in that ideal position, however. Sometimes parents, like teenagers, get confused about their priorities. Acne may be making your life miserable, or your pet may have died and left you distraught. Many parents won't remember how upsetting the same things were to them.

For Mark Duffet, friends are his sounding board. "My really good friends know that they can turn to me. That's the reason we are friends. We're there for each other, and not a lot of people have that. When I have a problem, I pick up the phone and have someone come over. I talk about it and get it out of my system and then we're on to the next thing."

There are many other routes you can take to get help. Use the one that feels easiest and most supportive. Choose someone who will not reassure you falsely. Someone who says, "You'll get through this okay" may not be telling the truth. By asking for help you are not giving up; rather, you are taking charge.

If peer counseling is available on an ongoing basis in your school, take advantage of it. Peer leaders are trained to help you solve problems; many of them will have had the same problem themselves. High schools and community mental-health centers will often have groups of students that meet to discuss a specific problem. For example, in one suburban Chicago high school a group meets to discuss the issues of having an alcoholic parent and another meets to advise pregnant teens.

Talk to someone you trust: the school psychologist, a guidance counselor, or a teacher. To help you cope with unusual problems at home, many high schools have crisis-intervention therapists. Ask to whom you can talk further about your problem, or ask if there is a specific place you can go for help. If you don't trust anyone in your school and your own parents are unapproachable, go to a relative or to a friend's mother or father. Seeking out a member of the clergy is another avenue for help. And don't shy away from hotlines. If you are afraid to call, have an adult or friend call for you.

Be sure you feel comfortable with the person you ultimately choose to talk with. It is much easier to explain yourself or your predicament if you are not worried about being judged or whether what you reveal will be kept confidential.

HELP CAN BE FAST

Many teenagers are resistant to seeking help. But help doesn't go on forever. The help offered to teenagers is designed to be practical and efficient so that you do not have to attend meetings or therapy sessions for a long time.

Too many teenagers believe that if they go anywhere for help they will be labeled crazy or that they are, in fact, crazy. Being unable to handle whatever must be faced happens to almost everyone at one time or another. Adults who help teenagers know better than anyone else that most people have problems but most people get through them, no matter what their age. Being in the midst of a difficult situation or feeling overwhelming distress is a far cry from being insane.

If you're confused or out of sorts about something, get some help for a short time. You'll be amazed at how talking a problem over with a trained person will bring out solutions and choices you hadn't even considered. The ability to talk about problems indicates maturity and a sense of confidence in oneself.

FEELING GOOD

People talk about self-confidence and self-esteem as if they were cereals, something packaged in a box to be plucked off a supermarket shelf. To complicate matters, the movie and advertising industries tell you that you are no good unless you wear a certain type of clothing or own a specific sports car by the time you're seventeen.

Too many parents wrongly think that they can raise their teenagers' self-esteem in a few weeks. Self-esteem is a whole way of being in the world. Unlike the techniques we have seen to reduce stress, you can't learn techniques to raise your self-image. You don't just get self-esteem from parents or friends telling you that you are a worthwhile individual. However, you do need feedback that you are a good person, that you do things well and your existence is valuable, but you have to live well to feel your own self-esteem.

The best way to develop self-esteem is to do things you are proud of. Become competent at something; be good to other people, be a good friend, care about someone you love. Helping a sibling, getting involved in a cause at school, or working at perfecting a sport are other ways to feel good about yourself. Concentrate on your strong suits and the things you have going for you. Examine what's going well at the moment. If something good has happened, pat yourself on the back and be proud.

On the other hand, it doesn't do any good to pretend you are not upset if you are. If your social life is getting you down, admit it to yourself. When things are in a mess, be nice to yourself. Stay calm, and think clearly. You can do this even if you're unhappy and under stress. Most people have too many problems to be able to deal with all of them at once. Attack one at a time. Don't cut off the people who might be able to help you or make you feel better. Stay involved with your friends and family.

You're old enough to form your own thoughts on life. By determining how you feel about drug use, war, teenage sex and pregnancy, abortion, violence, and success and failure you will develop guidelines for yourself. These may very well not be the same as your parents'. This doesn't mean that you have to stop loving them or that they don't love you.

Having your own set of rules and goals will be a big help not only in deciding what you want, but also in coping with any stress, anxiety, or depression you might encounter. Whenever your outlook seems extremely bleak, follow Drew Palmer's lead: "Right now I don't know what I'm going to do with my life, so I do my schoolwork, see my friends, and have as much fun as possible." Drew chooses not to be S.A.D. You can, too.

FINDING HELP

*I*mmediate medical attention can always be obtained at your hospital's emergency room. For the numbers of crisis centers in your vicinity, look in your local telephone directory or ask the operator for the Crisis Prevention Hotline number in your area. The police or your city's health department can also direct you to the services you need.

Listed below are the national offices and headquarters that can put you in touch with a local chapter or office of its organization. Telephone numbers change frequently, so if you don't get through, call 1-800-555-1212, an information service for toll-free telephone numbers.

AIDS

National AIDS Hotline
(800) 342-7514 (to speak with a counselor)
(800) 541-2437 (for recorded information)

American Red Cross
AIDS Education Office
1730 D Street
Washington, DC 20006
(202) 737-8000

EATING DISORDERS

American Anorexia/Bulimia Association
133 Cedar Lane
Teaneck, NJ 07666
(201) 836-1800

National Anorexic Aid Society
5796 Karl Road
Columbus, OH 43229
(614) 895-2009

National Association of Anorexia Nervosa and
  Associated Disorders

Box 7
Highland Park, IL 60035
(708) 831-3438

PHYSICAL ABUSE

National Child Abuse Hotline
(800) 4-A-CHILD
National Council on Child Abuse and Family Violence
(800) 222-2000
(818) 914-2814 in California

PREGNANCY AND ABORTION

National Abortion Federation Hotline
(800) 772-9100
Planned Parenthood Federation of America
810 Seventh Avenue
New York, NY 10019
(212) 541-7800

See the white pages of your telephone book for local listings for Birthright, Clergy Counseling Services, Crittenden Services (or the Florence Crittenden Association), or the National Organization of Women (NOW).

RUNAWAY AND HOMELESSNESS SOLUTIONS

Covenant House
(800) 999-9999
National Runaway Switchboard
(800) 621-4000
Runaway Hotline
(800) 231-6946
(800) 392-3352 from Texas

STRESS/ANXIETY/DEPRESSION

American Psychiatric Association
1400 K Street, N.W.
Washington, DC 20005
(202) 682-6000

Fair Oaks Hospital
19 Prospect Street

Summit, NJ 07901

(800) 526-4494 (for evaluation and direction)

Check local listings for Family and Child Services; Family Counseling Centers, Family Service Association of your county or city, Jewish Family Service, or United Family Service. Contact your local government department of health or department of human services.

SUBSTANCE ABUSE

Alcoholics Anonymous/Alateen (for teens who are affected by a
parent's drinking)
P.O. Box 459, Grand Central Station
New York, NY 10159
(212) 686-1100
Check phone directory for local listing.

Just Say No Foundation
1777 North California Blvd., Suite 210
Walnut, CA 94596
(800) 258-2766

National Association for Children of Alcoholics
31706 Coast Highway, Suite 201
South Laguna, CA 92677
(714) 499-3889

National Clearing House for Alcohol and Drug Information
P.O. Box 2345
Rockville, MD 20852
(301) 468-2600
(800) 729-6686

National Cocaine/Drug Abuse Hotline
(800) 262-2463

National Council on Alcoholism and Drug Dependence Hotline
(800) 622-2255

National Institute on Drug Abuse
P.O. Box 2305
Rockville, MD 20852
(301) 443-6245

SOURCES

Apter, Terri. *Altered Loves: Mothers and Daughters During Adolescence.* New York: St. Martin's, 1990.

Barden, J. C. "Toll of Troubled Families: Flood of Homeless Youths." *New York Times*, February 5, 1990.

Barringer, Felicity. "What IS Youth Coming To?" *New York Times*, August 19, 1990.

Berger, Joseph. "Condoms, AIDS and Morals: New Concern Alters Debate." *New York Times*, February 12, 1987.

Brody, Jane E. "For Millions of Sick Children, a Lifetime of Pain, Support and Understanding." *New York Times,* November 2, 1989.

———, "For Millions Who Are Shy, New Understanding of the Problem and Techniques for Overcoming It." *New York Times,* November 16, 1989.

Buder, Leonard. "Panel Hears Tales of Youth Violence." *New York Times,* January 31, 1990.

Burke, Kimberly Christie; Jack D. Burke; Darrel A. Regier; and Donald S. Rae. "Age at Onset of Selected Mental Disorders in Five Community Populations." *Archives of General Psychiatry.* 47 (1990): 511.

Burros, Marian. "Children Are Focus of Diet-Pill Issue." *New York Times,* October 3, 1990.

———. "Eating Well." *New York Times,* December 6, 1989.

Cauwels, Janice M. *Bulimia: The Binge-Purge Compulsion.* New York: Doubleday, 1983.

Chiles, John. *Teenage Depression and Suicide.* New York: Chelsea House, 1986.

Collins, Glen. "Study Says Teen-Agers Adopt Adult Values." *New York Times,* February 6, 1984.

Elkind, David. *All Grown Up & No Place to Go: Teenagers in Crisis.* Reading, Mass.: Addison-Wesley, 1984.

Fruchter, Rena. "Helping Women Battle Alcoholism." *New York Times,* August 19, 1990.

Goleman, Daniel. "Why Girls Are Prone to Depression." *New York Times,* May 10, 1990.

Gordon, Sol. *When Living Hurts.* New York: Union of American Hebrew Congregations, 1985.

_____ and Ruth Gordon. *Raising a Child Conservatively in a Sexually Permissive World.* New York: Simon & Schuster, 1983.

Gross, David A., and Irl L. Extein. *A Parent's Guide to Common and Uncommon School Problems.* Washington, D.C.: PIA Press, 1989.

Hall, Trish. "And Now, the Last Word on Dieting: Don't Bother." *New York Times,* January 3, 1990.

Johnson, Laurene, and Georglyn Rosenfeld. *Divorced Kids: What You Need to Know to Help Kids Survive a Divorce.* Nashville: Thomas Nelson, 1990.

Judd, Lewis A. "Study Finds Mental Disorders Strike Youngsters Earlier Than Thought." Hearing on Child and Adolescent Mental Disorders conducted by National Advisory Mental Health Council and the National Mental Health Leadership Forum, Los Angeles, Calif., October 9, 1990.

Kantrowitz, Barbara. "Kids and Contraceptives." *Newsweek,* February 16, 1987.

Klagsbrun, Francine. *Too Young to Die: Suicide and Youth.* Boston: Houghton Mifflin, 1976.

Kolata, Gina. "Bitter Dispute Is Threatening Program for Marrow Donors." *New York Times,* October 3, 1990.

_____. "Study Tells Why Alcohol Is Greater Risk to Women." *New York Times,* January 11, 1990.

Lucas, Alexander. "Early Detection and Intervention Strategies." Paper, Symposium on Adolescent Anxiety Disorders, New York, September 14, 1988.

McCoy, Kathleen. *Coping with Teenage Depression.* New York: New American Library, 1982.

Newman, Susan. *You Can Say No to a Drink or a Drug.* New York: Perigee/Putnam, 1986.

_____. *It Won't Happen to Me: True Stories of Teen Alcohol and Drug Abuse.* New York: Perigee/Putnam, 1987.

Newsweek. "The 21st Century Family." Special Ed. Winter/Spring 1990.

Offer, Daniel, Eric Ostrov, and Kenneth Howard. "The Mental Health Professional's Concept of the Normal Adolescent." *Archives of General Psychiatry* 38 (1981): 149.

O'Neill, Molly. "Congress Looking into the Diet Business." *New York Times,* March 28, 1990.

Orbach, Susie. *Fat Is a Feminist Issue.* New York: Berkley, 1978.

Rodgers, E. "Why Rape Often Is Committed by a Girl's Own Date, Boy Friend, or Fiancé—and What Can Be Done to Prevent It." *Seventeen,* March 1983, p. 36.

Rogan, Nina, and Maria Hussey. "The Development of a Life Change Events Scale for Adolescents." University of Cincinnati School of Nursing master's thesis, 1977.

Rosenbaum, Susan. "Schools Feel Impact of Children of Drug Abusers." *New York Times*, August 19, 1990.

Rosenthal, Elisabeth. "New Insights on Why Some Children Are Fat Offer Clues on Weight Loss." *New York Times*, January 4, 1990.

Seligmann, J. "The Date Who Rapes." *Newsweek*, April 9, 1984, p. 91.

Sherman, Eric. "Teenage Sex." *Ladies' Home Journal*, October 1986, p. 138.

Smilgis, Martha. "The Big Chill: Fear of AIDS." *Time*, February 16, 1987, p. 50.

Spence, Annette. *Stress and Mental Health.* New York: Facts on File, 1988.

Stein, Patricia M., and Barbara C. Unell. *Anorexia Nervosa: Finding the Life Line.* Minneapolis: CompCare Publications, 1986.

Valette, Brett. *A Parent's Guide to Eating Disorders: Prevention and Treatment of Anorexia Nervosa and Bulimia.* New York: Avon, 1988.

Ventura, Sylvia. "New Jersey Opinion: 8th-Grade Views on Society's Problems." Letter, *New York Times*, June 3, 1990.

Wallerstein, Judith S., and Sandra Blakeslee. *Second Chances: Men, Women and Children a Decade After Divorce.* New York: Ticknor & Fields, 1989.

Weissman, Myrna. "Prevalence and Risk: Genetic and Environmental Factors in Adolescent Anxiety." Paper, Symposium on Adolescent Anxiety Disorders, New York, September 14, 1988.

Wilson, Susan N., and Shirley Gordon. "Sex Education Declines, Teen-Age Births Rise." Letter, *New York Times*, September 12, 1990.

Zorn, Franny Heller. "Kids on the Couch: Therapy for Children Is on the Rise." *On The Avenue*, December 2, 1989.

FURTHER READING

Anastas, Robert. *The Contract for Life—The Story of S.A.D.D.* New York: Pocket Books, 1986.

Bell, Ruth. *Changing Bodies, Changing Lives.* Rev. ed. New York: Random House, 1987.

Cohen, Susan, and Daniel Cohen. *Teenage Stress.* New York: M. Evans, 1984.

Gordon, Barbara. *I'm Dancing as Fast as I Can.* New York: Bantam, 1980.

Gordon, James S., M.D. *Stress Management.* New York: Chelsea House, 1990.

Guernsey, JoAnn Bren. *(The Facts About) Teen Pregnancy.* New York: Crestwood House, 1989.

Guest, Judith. *Ordinary People.* New York: Viking, 1976.

Hales, Dianne. *Depression.* New York: Chelsea House, 1989.

Hoffman, Alice. *At Risk.* New York: Putnam, 1988.

Kirkland, Gelsey. *Dancing on My Grave.* New York: Jove, 1987.

Kolodny, Nancy; Robert Kolodny, and Thomas Bratter. *Smart Choices.* Boston: Little, Brown, 1986.

Krementz, Jill. *How It Feels to Fight for Your Life.* Boston: Joy Street/Little, Brown, 1989.

Landau, Elaine. *Why Are They Starving Themselves? Understanding Anorexia Nervosa & Bulimia.* New York: Julian Messner, 1983.

Lang, Alan R. *Alcohol: Teenage Drinking.* New York: Chelsea House, 1985.

Leach, Penelope. *Your Baby & Child: From Birth to Age Five.* New York: Knopf, 1985.

Levenkron, Steven. *The Best Little Girl in the World.* Chicago: Contemporary Books, 1978.

Madaras, Lynda. *Lynda Madaras Talks to Teens about AIDS.* New York: Newmarket, 1988.

Martin, Jo, and Kelly Clendenon. *Drugs & the Family.* New York: Chelsea House, 1988.

McCoy, Kathy, and Wibbelsman, Charles. *The New Teenage Body Book.* New York: Body Press/Price Stern Sloan, 1987.

McLellan, Tom; Alicia Bragg; and John Cacciola. *Escape from Anxiety and Stress.* New York: Chelsea House, 1986.

Newman, Susan. *It Won't Happen to Me: True Stories of Teen Alcohol and Drug Abuse.* New York: Perigee/Putnam, 1987.

Nourse, Alan E. *AIDS.* New York: Franklin Watts, 1986.

Poole, Victoria. *Thursday's Child.* Boston: Little, Brown, 1980.

Schnoll, Sidney. *Getting Help.* New York: Chelsea House, 1986.

Seixas, Judith S. *Living with a Parent Who Takes Drugs.* New York: Greenwillow, 1989.

Shaw, Diane. *Make the Most of a Good Thing: You! What You Need to Know about Exercise, Diet, Stress, Sexuality, Relationships & More.* Boston: Joy Street/Little, Brown, 1986.

Silverstein, Herma. *Teenage and Pregnant: What You Can Do.* Englewood Cliffs, N.J.: Julian Messner, 1988.

INDEX

ABOUT THE AUTHOR

Susan Newman is the author of several very successful books for teenagers, including *It Won't Happen to Me: True Stories of Teen Alcohol and Drug Abuse, You Can Say No to a Drink or a Drug: What Every Kid Should Know,* and *Never Say Yes to a Stranger: What Your Child Must Know to Stay Safe.* All three were produced as films/ videos by Simon & Schuster.